understand
basic business
finance

Philip Ramsden

flash.

Hodder Education is an Hachette UK company

First published in UK 2011 by Hodder Education.

This edition published 2011.

Copyright © Philip Ramsden

The moral rights of the author have been asserted.
Database right Hodder Education (makers).

British Library Cataloguing in Publication Data: a catalogue record for this title is available from the British Library.

10 9 8 7 6 5 4 3 2 1

The publisher has used its best endeavours to ensure that any website addresses referred to in this book are correct and active at the time of going to press. However, the publisher and the author have no responsibility for the websites and can make no guarantee that a site will remain live or that the content will remain relevant, decent or appropriate.

The publisher has made every effort to mark as such all words which it believes to be trademarks. The publisher should also like to make it clear that the presence of a word in the book, whether marked or unmarked, in no way affects its legal status as a trademark.

Every reasonable effort has been made by the publisher to trace the copyright holders of material in this book. Any errors or omissions should be notified in writing to the publisher, who will endeavour to rectify the situation for any reprints and future editions.

Hachette UK's policy is to use papers that are natural, renewable and recyclable products and made from wood grown in sustainable forests. The logging and manufacturing processes are expected to conform to the environmental regulations of the country of origin.

www.hoddereducation.co.uk

Typeset by MPS Limited, a Macmillan Company.
Printed in Great Britain by CPI Cox & Wyman, Reading.

Contents

1

the purpose of accounting

Despite being maligned from time to time, accountancy is a necessary part of business. So this chapter serves as a general introduction as to why the need for accounting came about, what basic information is needed, and why it has become the major activity it is today. Hopefully, this will help explain why accountants ask people to sign off invoices and produce Goods Received Notes, say – not for the sake of it, but to help them do their job.

If you were asked to name the principal objective of a company, would you say that it is to make money?

It's a common reply to the question and, for most companies, it is the main reason for their existence, although there are, of course, those organizations that are non-profit making.

One thing all businesses have in common is the need to measure that profit, or surplus, in order to know that they are, in fact, making one. But profit arises from making hundreds, thousands, even millions of business transactions – buying, selling, moving, packing, storing ...

Recording transactions

To be able to measure the profits (or losses), these transactions have to be recorded, if they have a monetary value. What use is a salesperson who, when asked 'How much did you sell that Jaguar for?', gives the answer 'I don't know, but I did manage to sell it.'? You wouldn't know if a profit had been made on the deal, the sum to be collected from the customer, whether it would be enough to pay the manufacturer or what the salesperson's commission (or termination payment) should be.

Just because transactions and results are measured in Dollars or Pounds or Euros or Yen, notes and coins do not necessarily change hands every time a transaction is made. It would slow commercial activity to a snail's pace if we all had to pay as we go, so the business world operates largely on credit – take these goods now and pay me in 30 days please. But the transaction needs to be recorded, to remind the customer to pay, and you to ask him if he doesn't.

It becomes more complicated because, when you sell a product, not only do you need to remember to ask for the money later, you must also deduct the product from your stock records. Otherwise you (or your computer) might think you've still got it and try to sell it again.

Such is the volume of transactions in modern companies that whole departments are needed to handle them. Usually, Sales Order Processing administers the orders from customers served by sales representatives out in the field. Production schedulers shuffle alternatives to get sufficient product into stock to meet delivery deadlines. Buyers co-ordinate purchases and deliveries between production requirements and suppliers' lead times. And back in the offices, the Accounts department keeps track of the financial implications of all that goes on elsewhere.

Accounting

What is the difference between an Accounts department and a Finance department? Nothing, it's just that some companies like to call it Accounts, and others prefer Finance.

When businesses were literally one-man operations, and the owner did all the selling and buying, he also kept his own records – how much he paid for his bushels, what he had sold them for, how many he had left at the end of the day.

Two changes in the commercial world meant things could not go on that way. The first was that enterprises started getting bigger, so that one person couldn't do everything. The owner needed partners or employees, although he could still take a dominant role in the proceedings. But it meant some tasks had to be delegated, and who wants to get stuck with the administration when they can give it to someone else?

Having a partner meant having to share the profits of the business, so the first step was to work out what those profits were. It hadn't been as important when Giovanni Peluga was the sole proprietor of his Florentine market stall – he could tell by the cash in his pocket whether he was doing all right or not. But when he had to divide it up with his partner Luigi Constantino, he wanted to be sure he was getting his fair share. So a methodology was needed to work out what that would be.

The definitive work

This was provided by a treatise on mathematics and associated subjects by the Franciscan monk Luca Pacioli, which was published in 1495.

Pacioli has two claims to fame. The first is that he collaborated with Leonardo da Vinci on a number of projects, being considered a man of high intellect himself. Secondly, his work *Summa de arithmetica, geometria proportioni et proportionalita* (to use its short name) formed the basis of accounting rules that are the underlying foundation of current finance techniques.

This is not to say that Pacioli invented accountancy or that the subject has not changed over the past five hundred years. Pacioli himself wrote in the book that the rules he was putting forward were considered best practice by the traders in northern Italy, particularly in Florence where he was based at the time. His work was the first recording in considerable detail of the principles of bookkeeping.

These basic principles, still intact in modern accounting, are as follows:
* that all transactions should be recorded in great detail in a book called the *memorandum*
* the transactions should then be transferred to another book, the *ledger*, and that each transaction has at least two entries to it, a debit and a credit, hence the term 'double entry bookkeeping'.

There's nothing difficult about writing things down and then writing them down somewhere else in a different order, but accountants appear to have turned a simple task into a black art in the eyes of many managers from other disciplines and functions!

Accounting grows up

The second big impact on commerce came when enterprises started to get so big that they needed capital from outside investors. With managers running the company, a distinction developed between owners and managers. This separation is normal for the plcs of today but, when it first became common, the owners had to rely on reports from the management to let them know how their company was performing. They still do.

Now suppose, back in the early part of the twentieth century, you had invested £10,000 in a textile mill operation. Three months go by and you want to know how the business is doing.

When the year-end reports come from the mill manager, they back up what he's been saying throughout the year and you get your nice little dividend, as promised. Leaving the meeting when all the figures were announced, you notice the manager has replaced his car with another new one, the latest sporty number.

Suspicious? Why should you be? The reports from the manager confirm everything he's told you. But you've no doubt spotted the flaw – he prepares the reports!

Investors thought they needed protecting from unscrupulous managers: at best they may be hiding poor performance; at worst they may be acting fraudulently and stealing from the company (and therefore from the investors). Several notorious cases only confirmed the urgent need to introduce an independent check that would instil investor confidence. This type of check is called an audit.

The greater need for more knowledge

Given the importance of financial awareness for managers from all disciplines, the need to be familiar with the methods, concepts and principles of the world of accounting is strong. Even armed with some basic knowledge – or perhaps only with numerous assumptions – many managers still do not believe that a profitable company can actually go bust. But it can. Some circumstances surrounding a company might, at first glance, suggest that all is well. Considered observation of the company's accounts by someone with an educated eye might suggest or reveal something different.

2

basic terminology, concepts and principles

Like any profession, accountants have a terminology peculiar to themselves, so let's address some of this straightaway. You'll need to know what the three main financial reports are, and it's always useful if you can follow accountants when they talk about 'debiting and crediting the general ledger', which is so simple in practice, it needs a bit of jargon to make it sound exciting. A quick look at this ledger and others follows, then an explanation of a few of more buzzwords – 'accrual' and 'prepayments', neither as complicated as they sound. Soon you will be dropping these words into conversation at work yourself ...

It can't be avoided indefinitely, though; at some point knowing the words isn't going to be enough, you need to know what they actually mean. This chapter is going to enlighten you on double entry bookkeeping, and once you've grasped the idea of debit and credit, you will have no problem with this. Then we'll revisit the accruals idea, because accountants like that one a lot, then historic cost, then wrap up with the difference between profit and cash. That's a key one.

Basic terminology

Accounting jargon is much like that of any other specialist subject – it makes a quick reference to longer expressions, but is handy to use when you know what the words mean.

The accounts

In business talk, 'the accounts' implies the set of reports that shows the financial standing of the company. Specifically, there are three major reports:

1 the Profit & Loss Account
2 the Balance Sheet
3 the Cash Flow Statement.

In a less formal discussion, the accounts refer to the system of recording and reporting the financial implications of the company's activities. The key system is the general ledger, which is composed of a number of accounts in a structure appropriate to the nature of the organization. The general ledger is the financial 'bucket' into which all the financial transactions of the company are poured.

The accounts, for those composing the general ledger, can designate different levels of reporting within the business, e.g. type of cost, department, cost centre, division. Usually an account code identifies each element uniquely, particularly if the general ledger is on a computer. For instance these types of cost may be coded as follows:

Electricity	*U200*
Gas	*U210*
Oil	*U220*
Water	*U230*

Similar types of expenditure should be grouped together under one code to make summaries easier to construct, as in the above example: all utilities expenditures start with a U, and the number part of each code is related to the others. A gap of 10 is usually used so new codes can be inserted as required.

A general ledger code may appear as **200/U210** meaning the electricity cost (U210) for cost centre 200 (which might stand for production), or it could look like this: **014726A3964002**.

Although it might not be obvious, the general ledger code always has a consistent structure. In the second case it might be:

first 2 characters	–	*company code*
next 4	–	*division code*
next 5	–	*profit centre*
next 3	–	*expense type*

The chart of accounts will list all valid codes for each segment of the total code.

Debits and credits

Debits and credits are the nuts and bolts of accounting but, essentially they are just the financial equivalent of 'plus' and 'minus'.

Financial transactions are recorded in money and 'signed' with minus for a debit or plus for a credit. For any given transaction or series of transactions, the overriding rule is that the sum of the debits must equal the sum of the credits.

This means that, mathematically, the net effect on the total accounts is nil, since total debits will equal total credits. This implies that the general ledger (where all transactions are effectively stored as debits and credits) will always sum to zero and the Balance Sheet, produced on the basis of the general ledger, must, as the name suggests, balance.

Just to give you a flavour of how debits and credits apply in practice (there will be many more examples to follow), here is the accounting for paying a maintenance bill of £1,000, settled in cash:

Debit	Maintenance costs £1,000
Credit	Cash £1,000

Generally debits indicate an expense, or adding to an asset (e.g. stock). Credits indicate gains (typically sales) or increases in liabilities (e.g. trade creditors).

The balancing nature of a transaction must be emphasized, no matter how many general ledger codes it affects. For example, a single gas bill for a site might be allocated to a number of cost centres:

Production	Debit	£3,000
Administration	Debit	£500
Warehouse	Debit	£1,200
Creditors	Credit	£4,700 (gas supplier's account)

Similarly, the routine invoicing of a sale could be described like this:

Debtors	Debit	£6,000
Sales	Credit	£5,000
Output VAT	Credit	£1,000

Ledgers

Originally this term referred to the actual books in which the transactions and the accounts were recorded. Although accounts are now usually kept on computers rather than in 16-column ledger books, the principles remain the same. The main ledgers are the:

* **sales** (or debtors) **ledger**, which shows how much is owed to the company by each customer; the balance on each customer's account is generated from sales made to the customer less payments received.
* **purchase** (or creditors) **ledger**, which shows how much the company owes to its suppliers; these balances are derived from invoices from the supplier for goods or services rendered, less any payments made to the supplier.
* **general** (or nominal) **ledger**, which contains records of the financial implications of the company's transactions. Depending upon the number and nature of transactions, they may be recorded in summary form rather than in detail, although reporting systems will hopefully allow analysis of any summarized transactions into their constituent parts.

The difficulty with detailed posting (making entries in the ledgers) is that an enquiry into what has been posted may reveal that thousands of transactions make up the total. If the accountant is looking for a transaction made in error (say the sales account reads £10,000,000 when it should be £1,000,000), she would have to wade through reams of lists in the hope of finding the offending transaction. If summary postings were made daily, she could soon identify which batch looked unusually large and use the sales system to list just that day's transactions.

The general ledger is the primary source of financial information in the preparation of the Profit & Loss Account and the Balance Sheet. How the general ledger connects with the other two principal ledgers, and everything else, is disclosed later.

Accounting period

This is a notional period for recording and reporting the financial results for a given time. The usual accounting period in the UK is one year, since limited companies are legally required to prepare and submit annual accounts to Companies House, where they become available for public inspection.

The management of the company will not, of course, want to wait a year to find out what's going on. For purposes internal to the company, the financial year is broken down into shorter accounting periods. There are usually either 13 periods of four weeks each, or 12 periods based either on calendar months or with a repeated pattern of 4–4–5 weeks. There is no best method, just what suits the organization, but be aware that if the company is using the 4–4–5 split it is essential to make comparisons between periods of the same length – an increase in sales figures can look very good if there are five weeks in a particular period against four in another.

Prepayments and accruals

A prepayment is an amount paid in advance but which is not deducted from the profits of the company until the time to which it relates arrives. Insurance is a good example – if the premium for the year ahead is £20,000 and this has to be paid at the start of the year, that cost should be spread over the whole financial year. After six months, £10,000 will have been charged to the Profit & Loss Account, leaving the other £10,000 as a prepayment shown in the Balance Sheet. In this way, the cost is spread over the relevant periods.

An accrual is the opposite of a prepayment. Rent for a site may be paid three months in arrears, but that doesn't mean the first two months are free! If the payment is £7,500 a quarter, then £2,500 rent should be charged to the Profit & Loss Account each month. Until the invoice for the rent is actually received or the rent paid, this amount is an accrual. The concept of accruals is explained in more detail later in this chapter.

Journal voucher

Most real transactions are initiated by a piece of paper. A sales invoice imparts the relevant information. So on the one hand, we can increase the reported sales figure by £5,000 and, on the other, the debtors by the same amount.

Some transactions which affect the company can be more apparent than real. For instance, someone whose wages are normally charged to the Inspection department has been helping out in the warehouse. So, for this month, his manager wants that wage cost to be charged to the warehouse instead. One way of doing this would be to change the payroll system so that all costs relating to this man are charged to the warehouse. Then when he's finished his warehouse stint, the records can be reset to charge the Inspection department in future. This is messy for short-term changes.

What would normally happen is that the payroll information would go into the general ledger, possibly by an automatic transfer (interface) on the computer. This would allocate all the wage costs against the usual departments, as held on the payroll system. To move the cost from one department to another, an Accounts person with the proper authority would 'enter a journal'. This apparent sleight of hand involves no more than filling out a form (a journal voucher) showing which parts of the general ledger are to be debited (cost increased) and which credited. Depending upon the structure of the general ledger, each department has its own code and the journal is merely the transfer of amounts between places in the general ledger.

Please note that doing this does not reduce the overall wage cost to the company, it merely transfers a cost from one department to another!

Budget

The budget is a plan of what the management hopes or expects the company to achieve. It normally covers a financial year, broken down into shorter accounting periods. Actual results are reported against the budget to allow the management to measure the company's progress. The budget can also include sales and production volumes to whatever level of detail (product and/or customer) the management considers appropriate.

Audit trail

This simply allows anyone, including auditors, to trace the source of any reported transaction. It is used as a check on the security and integrity of the reporting systems, to make sure that they include all transactions in the period and that no extraneous ones have crept in.

So a payment to a supplier should be capable of being traced back to the cash book and the bank statement, and should be supported by an invoice, proof of delivery of the goods and possibly even a purchase order.

Reconciliation of accounts

This refers to the check that is made on the integrity of different parts of the system. The main recording and reporting system is the general ledger, but the initial transactions are often recorded first in other ledgers and systems, principally the sales and purchase ledgers.

There will exist in the general ledger two accounts: the sales ledger control account and the purchase ledger control account. If the balances of these agree with the balances of the debtors and creditors ledger respectively, then all is in harmony.

The sales ledger has separate accounts for each customer, each of those being made up of that customer's invoices less credits notes and payments received. It is the total of all these accounts which should be represented in the sales ledger control account in the general ledger. The principle also applies to the purchase ledger.

Other reconciliations include balancing:

* the cash book to the bank statement
* general ledger payroll accounts to the payroll figures
* other debtors and creditors, such as rates and insurance which may be prepayments or accruals.

Accounting concepts and principles

Double entry bookkeeping

The foundation of accounting and finance is double entry bookkeeping. The underlying principle is that all recorded transactions must affect at least two, but possibly more, accounts. As mentioned in Chapter 1, this is an old concept, but it has not been radically altered over the past five hundred years. By following the practices recommended by Luca Pacioli all those years ago, accountants can still ensure that their Balance Sheets always balance.

Every transaction has two or more entries in the general ledger. Here's an example based on buying stock. The debit and credit entries are abbreviated to dr and cr. The stock is bought for £1,000 on 30 days' credit and the first transaction would read:

	Dr	Cr	(meaning)
Stock	£1,000		(we have the stock)
Creditors		£1,000	(we owe someone for it)

And when the bill is paid the transaction would read:

	Dr	Cr	(meaning)
Creditors	£1,000		(pay what is owed so that the creditors' balance becomes nil)
Cash		£1,000	(reduce the cash balance)

It is only slightly more complicated if the supplier is registered for VAT (as most are) and, therefore, is obliged to add the tax to the charges at the rate of 20%:

	Dr	Cr	(meaning)
Stock	£1,000		
Input VAT	£200		(reclaimable from HM Revenue and Customs)
Creditors		£1,200	

This is a transaction with three accounting entries, but you will notice that, as always, the entries do balance – the sum of the debits equals the sum of the credits, in this case, £1,200.

When the bill is paid, the entries look like this:

	Dr	Cr
Creditors	£1,200	
Cash		£1,200

The VAT account will be cleared when the VAT is settled at the end of the VAT period, which is usually either monthly or quarterly.

Note that the example above concerned accounts in the Balance Sheet, since the company has not yet done anything to create a profit or loss. It has merely swapped one asset (cash) for another (stock). Now consider the selling side – £900 worth of stock sells for £1,600 plus VAT, which at 20% adds a further £320 to the invoice.

The transaction is described in two parts. First deal with the customer:

	Dr	Cr	(meaning)
Debtors	£1,920		(how much we are owed)
Sales		£1,600	(in the Profit and Loss Account)
Output VAT		£320	(due to HM Revenue and Customs)

And now with the stock used:

	Dr	Cr	(meaning)
Cost of sales	£900		(in the Profit and Loss Account)
Stock		£900	(reduce the stock balance)

Just as a brief aside, traditionally the debit transactions are shown first, but it doesn't make any difference really.

Taking the two previous examples together (using the VAT-rated supplier of the stock and before the supplier is paid or the customer pays up), a set of accounts can be drawn up. This is based on the total entries to each account (stock, sales, etc.) that have been made and the final balance that results from the sum of all the transactions. So, for instance, the general ledger for the stock account will look like this:

	Stock	
	Dr	Cr
Purchase	£1,000	
Sold		£900

The transaction leaves a closing balance on the stock account of £100.

In addition, you would normally also see the dates of the transactions and other relevant details, such as who the supplier and customer were and which products were bought and sold. In the accounts, it is not usually practical to keep a stock account for each product line – there could be thousands of them. That level of detail is found in the stock control system. All the accounts usually show are the total value of stock, perhaps with a split between raw materials, work in progress and finished goods.

Anyway, back to our example and the complete accounts based on the two transactions we've had so far.

Profit and Loss Account	
	£
Sales	1,600
Cost of sales	900
Profit	700

Balance Sheet		
	£	
Stock	100	
Debtors	1,920	
Creditors	(1,200)	
VAT due	(120)	(= 200 – 320)
Cash	–	
Net Assets	700	
Current profit	700	

The Balance Sheet balances, as it must always do. Note in particular:

* The debit/credit balance of each account is not stated in the formal presentation of the results.
* The debit and credits are inferred in the Profit and Loss Account rather than specified, although sometimes the sales, or indeed the cost of sales, can be shown in brackets to identify that debits and credits have different signs.
* The current profit in the Balance Sheet is the direct link to the profit figure from the Profit and Loss Account.

* In the Balance Sheet, the use of brackets to represent credit balances is more common. However, since debtors is invariably a debit balance and creditors a credit one, brackets are often omitted and left to the assumed knowledge of the reader!

Here's a quick look at what happens when the customer pays the £1,920 and the company settles with its supplier with a payment of £1,200 – or if you feel you've got the hang of this, try to construct the Balance Sheet yourself.

Profit and Loss Account	
	£
Sales	1,600
Cost of sales	900
Profit	700

Balance Sheet		
	£	
Stock	100	
Debtors	–	
Creditors	–	
VAT due	(120)	(= 200 – 320)
Cash	720	(= 1,920 – 1,200)
Net Assets	700	
Current profit	700	

Cash, debtors and creditors all change, but the Balance Sheet still balances!

Note that the Profit and Loss Account doesn't change at all when payments are made or received, because nothing has happened which would create a profit or a loss – assets and liabilities have only changed form (debtors to cash received, creditors to cash paid). Cash is not the same as profit, a point which will be emphasized shortly.

In double entry bookkeeping, if you make sure that each individual transaction balances (all the debits equal all the credits), no matter how complicated the transactions might appear, and no matter how many of them there are, in the end the Balance Sheet must balance too.

Cash v. accruals

Possibly the most important concept in accounting is the distinction between cash transactions and 'accruals'. Put in accounting parlance, the accrual concept matches the transaction to the accounting period in which it occurs, not when cash payment is subsequently made or received. In plainer English, accountants want to reflect in their accounts for a particular accounting period all the things that happened during that period, without waiting for the resulting cash side of things to catch up.

Consider the previous purchase of stock, excluding the VAT to start with. The stock is acquired in January, but on 60 days' credit terms. So payment is not due until March. Even so, we want to recognize that the purchase has been incurred in January and so it is included in January's accounts. We can't pretend that, just because we don't have to pay for the goods until March, we didn't have them until then.

Hence the transactions recorded in the ledgers are:

January		£	March		£
Stock	**Dr**	1,000	**Creditors**	**Dr**	1,000
Creditors	**Cr**	1,000	**Cash**	**Cr**	1,000

Normally, a supplier would submit a purchase invoice for the goods when the items are delivered, or very soon afterwards. This is usually the document that triggers the recognition that a financial transaction has been incurred.

However, if the supplier does not actually send an invoice along with the goods or by the time the entries for the accounting period are closed, it does not mean that the organization can pretend that the stock either never arrived or was free. Instead of putting the credit entry into the creditors account, a more general one called 'goods received not invoiced' (GRNI) is used. The GRNI account would appear in the current liabilities section of the Balance Sheet, close to the creditors, since it represents much the same thing – it's what the company owes someone for goods or services provided.

Depending upon the control systems that the company has in place for monitoring such activities, it is likely that a goods received note, filled in by the Goods Receiving or Warehouse department, would be the main document for Accounts to use for this purpose.

The key point is to recognize and reflect in the accounts all financial transactions in the accounting period in which they occur, not when the paperwork catches up. The technical term for this is the accruals concept, as opposed to cash accounting. Small businesses (very small ones) may prefer to use cash accounting, which only recognizes transactions when they are resolved in cash – a sale is not perceived as such until the cash is received from the customer. Bear in mind this could be several months after the event took place.

Accruals are an important idea in accounting. Just because we haven't paid for it doesn't mean we haven't had it or used it, so an accrual is made, a charge (debit) to the accounts as if we have had the invoice. So where does the credit entry go? An account in the liabilities section of the Balance Sheet, called 'GRNI' or even 'Accruals'.

So, when accountants say they will accrue for something, all they mean is that the paperwork for this transaction hasn't come through for it yet, but they will make an adjustment to the accounts *as if it had*. The adjustment is made with a journal voucher posted to the general ledger.

Historic cost

All the figures in accounts are prepared based on historic cost, which simply means the cost of the thing at the time it was incurred. Normally this is not a particular problem – if a sale was made in January of 10 tonnes of lead at £400 a tonne, then the sales and debtors accounts show £4,000, even if the price of lead moves to £500 in February (lead is a commodity with a fluctuating price). Figures are not restated, but kept at what they were when the transaction took place. There are two possible exceptions to this.

Stock is valued at the lower of cost or net realizable value

Invariably, this leads to stock being valued at cost – what the organization paid for it at the time it acquired it – because the intention is to sell the stock at more than it cost. However, changing market circumstances may mean that this is impossible (the product may be obsolete or perhaps be a market commodity whose price has fallen). On such occasions, it is deemed prudent to revalue the stock at how much it *could* be sold for – the net realizable cost. 'Net' simply means after the transport or handling charges needed to dispose of the stock.

However, because of the nature of most items held in stock and the way in which stock is sold, it can occasionally be revalued. When stock is valued at standard cost this occurs usually annually, if not more often. Revaluation will occur when actual costs, that the company is paying out to suppliers, have changed significantly from the standard costs used to value the stock.

The other exception is to do with fixed assets

Imagine that a company purchased its headquarters 30 years ago for £100,000. If the building were to be depreciated over 50 years, the current net book value (the original cost less accumulated depreciation) of the building in the accounts would be £40,000 (depreciation is calculated at £2,000 a year for 30 years = £60,000, deducted from the original cost to give the net book value). Depending upon its location, the building is not only likely to be worth more than that if sold, but even more than was paid for it in the first place. This leads to the obvious conclusion that accounts ignore inflation – they do. Attempts have been made to replace historic cost accounting with current cost accounting, but generally these have created more problems than they have solved.

Back to the building which, following depreciation, has been accounted for 'in the books' at just £40,000. It is permissible for the directors, with the advice of professionals (usually chartered surveyors), to revalue the fixed assets in the accounts. Assume these fine headquarters could now fetch £500,000 if sold. Does that mean the organization can add a windfall £460,000 to its profits for the year?

The accounts have to be made to balance. If fixed assets are to be restated upwards by £460,000, what is the other entry? The answer is the creation of a revaluation reserve in the equity part of the Balance Sheet, rather than adding to the current profitability of the company. The sensible logic behind this is that the apparent gain is only a notional one until the building is actually sold. It would be foolish to pretend that an organization is making healthy profits when all it is doing is occupying a building whose value increases every year. As a safeguard, there is a legal prevention from distributing the revaluation reserve as part of the dividend payment to the shareholders, since it is not a real profit.

So why revalue fixed assets? Only to reflect more accurately the value of the assets of the company as stated in the balance sheet.

The alternative to using the historic cost convention presents a great dilemma to the accountancy world. The problem arises from the fact that historic costs do not, by definition, reflect the real, up-to-date, intrinsic value of the assets on a company's Balance Sheet. Thus, if investors and potential investors (including other companies who might want to take it over) use the accounts to form the basis of their investment strategy, they might not get an accurate picture of the true worth of the company's assets.

Statement of Standard Accounting Practice, number 16, recommended that various figures in the Balance Sheet should be restated at replacement cost values, but this was eventually withdrawn after much controversy.

The main figures that would be affected by such a rule are the stock and the fixed assets. Debtors and creditors wouldn't change – if a customer owes £8,000, all you'll ever get is £8,000, no matter when he pays. On the other hand, stock may cost more to replace now than when it was bought, since prices tend to rise rather than fall. Revaluing the stock at replacement cost rather than historic increases the asset value of the company and, to make the whole thing balance, the profits must rise by the same amount. Of course, in reality, nothing has happened. The same quantity of stock is still there, so this is merely a paper increase in value, a trick of accountancy. It is easy to see why it fell into disrepute.

No alternative method has yet been proposed successfully.

Profit v. cash

Although we have already discussed the accruals concept – that the accounts reflect activities which have occurred and not just those backed by the exchange of cash – it is important to stress the difference between profit and cash.

It is perfectly feasible for a company to go bust while it is making profits. Indeed, this is the most common cause of failure among start-up businesses. An example will show why. Consider the first few months of trading for Aardvark Overseas Limited, a company supplying statues of exotic animals.

	Jan	Feb	Mar	Apr	May
Sales (£)	5,000	7,000	10,000	15,000	18,000
Purchases (£)	7,000	8,000	6,000	10,000	10,000
Overheads (£)	2,000	2,000	2,000	2,000	2,000

Obviously, the company has some stock left at the end of each month, but first let's calculate the profit, assuming that the company makes a gross margin of 40% on its sales (which is the same as saying the cost of sales is 60% of the sales value).

So in January, sales are £5,000. Therefore, the cost of sales is 60% × £5,000 = £3,000, leaving a gross margin of £2,000. Then the closing stock for January is worked out by:

Opening stock	–
Purchases (£)	7,000
Cost of sales (COS) (£)	(3,000)
Closing stock (£)	4,000

That is: what we started with
plus: what was bought
less: what was used
giving: what's left.

The stock position for all the months looks like this:

	Jan	Feb	Mar	Apr	May
Opening (£)	–	4,000	7,800	7,800	8,800
Purchases (£)	7,000	8,000	6,000	10,000	10,000
COS (£)	(3,000)	(4,200)	(6,000)	(9,000)	(10,800)
Closing (£)	4,000	7,800	7,800	8,800	8,000

(Note that the closing stock for one month becomes the opening stock for the next and that the cost of sales in each month is 60% of sales.)

We can now put together a Profit and Loss Account:

	Jan	Feb	Mar	Apr	May
Sales (£)	5,000	7,000	10,000	15,000	18,000
COS (£)	(3,000)	(4,200)	(6,000)	(9,000)	(10,800)
Gross margin (£)	2,000	2,800	4,000	6,000	7,200
Overheads (£)	(2,000)	(2,000)	(2,000)	(2,000)	(2,000)
Profit (£)	–	800	2,000	4,000	5,200

That's a total of £12,000 profit in five months and improving all the time after a slow start.

Let us suppose, however, that because this is a new business venture, the company finds it difficult to get credit for its supplies, since it has no track record for paying out. It has to pay its suppliers the following month after the goods are received, but all overheads (salaries, rent, etc.) are paid in the month in which they are incurred. Also, to attract customers, it offers to give them credit of three months, so sales in January are paid for in April. Assuming the company started off with £10,000 in cash (from the shareholders), the cash flow looks like this:

	Jan	Feb	Mar	Apr	May
Opening (£)	10,000	8,000	(1,000)	(11,000)	(14,000)
Receipts (£)	–	–	–	5,000	7,000
Payments:					
Suppliers (£)	–	(7,000)	(8,000)	(6,000)	(10,000)
Overheads (£)	(2,000)	(2,000)	(2,000)	(2,000)	(2,000)
Closing (£)	8,000	(1,000)	(11,000)	(14,000)	(19,000)

(Note that April's receipts are from sales in January. Payments to suppliers in February are from January's purchases.)

Thereafter, the cash position improves (feel free to extend the cash flow yourself), but at the worst point, the company needs to find another source of funding for £19,000. A simple bank overdraft may do it, but there may not be a bank willing to lend to what may seem a risky enterprise. Yet all the time, the company is profitable. So a profit does not automatically mean a cash surplus.

It is a lack of cash and the resulting inability to finance its operations that leads to the downfall of many companies, rather than a lack of profit. Just imagine how much worse it would have been if the company had been making losses during its first few months, while it became established!

3

the three major financial accounts

Most people's introduction to accounting is hearing about a company making x billions of pounds (or losing it). That highlight of information comes from the Profit & Loss Account, so we might as well know what's in the rest of it, so we can see how that profit (or loss) came about. We will spend more time on depreciation, because that one seems to confuse people as much as anything does.

Often neglected by the media, who are interested in sensationalizing the size of a company's profit or loss, the Balance Sheet gives a better idea of a company's value, and indeed, its size. Like the Profit & Loss Account, it is broken down into sections, and they are all reasonably straightforward too.

The Cash Flow Statement is also a key document. Despite the apparently complicated way in which the report is often presented, the ideas behind it are pretty simple, and generally involve no more than looking at how much a company has sold compared to how much of it has actually been paid for by customers, and the opposite – how much it has bought and paid for.

The three major financial reports are the Profit and Loss Account, the Balance Sheet and the Cash Flow Statement.

All limited companies are required by law to produce an annual set of accounts, in a prescribed format. These will contain a Profit and Loss (P&L) Account, a Balance Sheet and a Cash Flow Statement, together with notes to the accounts which explain some of the detail behind the numbers and some further explanation of the accounting policies used to determine them.

These statutory accounts, as they are called, are available from Companies House, which has its main office in Cardiff, with other offices around the UK.

The profit and loss account

A P&L Account for use by the company's management will have more detail than the one in the statutory accounts. Not only that, but the numbers can be different too! The reason is that one version of the P&L Account tells the managers how profitably they have run the company, but the one published in the statutory accounts may contain 'adjustments' which, although technically valid, give the management some leeway on what they wish to publicly report.

This is not to suggest that the published profitability is in any way false or made up; rather, the management can take advantage of some accountancy 'tricks' to adjust the reported profit in either direction. One example is capitalization of interest.

Say a retail company is building a new store. The cost is £10m. The finished store becomes a fixed asset in the company's accounts, at a cost of £10m. But suppose, instead of paying cash for the building, the company borrowed from the bank and paid say £2m in interest charges, what is the cost of the building now? Some companies would add that £2m to the asset value of the building. The alternative would be to reduce the profits of the company by £2m by charging the interest to the profits. So we have a building that can be valued at either £10m or £12m, but it's the same building!

This accounting adjustment would not interest the company's managers in the first instance. They would want to know what the 'real' profit is – what the company has achieved under their direction. Once that is established, they leave any further adjustments to the accountants who will try to convince the auditors of the merits of the adjustments. So, we will concentrate on what the management would find useful in a P&L Account. In other companies, the same report may be referred to as an income statement or an operating results statement. Broadly, these are the same thing, although the level of detail may vary.

A P&L Account format for management use may look like this:

P&L Account for the year ending 31 March 2011	£000s	£000s
Sales		34,252
Cost of sales:		
Materials	10,429	
Labour	4,731	
Direct costs	3,390	
Total cost of sales		18,550
Gross profit		15,702
GP %		45.8%
Overheads:		
Staff costs	5,630	
Indirect costs	4,350	
Depreciation	1,422	
Total overheads		11,402
Profit before interest and tax		4,300
Interest:		
Receivable	112	
Payable	604	
Net interest		492
Profit before tax		3,808

For management purposes, the P&L Account is not likely to go as far as showing tax, since this is largely an area beyond the management's control, being a specialist subject in its own right. That does not mean it should be ignored, because good tax planning can save companies a considerable amount of money, but professional advice is usually taken in this respect. The management would expect to receive monthly reports on the company's profitability with the appropriate analysis, perhaps with a year-to-date column and a comparison against a budget or plan. Let's consider each line in the P&L Account in detail and what it actually represents.

Sales – this is the amount, excluding VAT, invoiced to customers for goods or services rendered. The sales figure is always shown without VAT, because eventually this has to be paid over to HM Revenue and Customs, so it has no effect on the company's profit. The figure will normally be the full invoice amount before any allowances for discounts or early payment settlements. For instance, we could charge Edison Lighthouses Limited £5,000 (before VAT) for products, but the terms under which we trade may offer them a 5% discount if they pay within seven days. Whether they pay in seven days and take the discount or not, the sales figure remains the same: £5,000. Any discounts taken are usually charged to a Discounts line in the overheads section.

Credit notes issued to customers (for goods rejected or invoicing errors) are deducted from the sales figure, so that the net figure is shown after all credits.

Cost of sales – as it seems to indicate, this is the cost to the company of making and/or supplying the products that were invoiced to the customers. If the company does not have a standard costing system then it can use actual costs in the following simple manner. Depending on how the costing structure of the products is set out, up to three elements are commonly found, although they are not always split in the Profit and Loss Account:

1 Working out the *cost of materials* becomes a simple mathematical exercise. Add to the opening stock (the stock value at the start of the accounting period) the value of products purchased during the period to give a subtotal of stock available for sale. Subtract from that the closing stock value (the stock value at the end of the period) and you must be left

with what was used. This becomes the cost of sales. Theoretically, the figure is distorted by any stock adjustments (i.e. shrinkage or damaged stock), but they will have to be 'written off' at some point, since they would be no longer saleable.

(NB The term 'written off', much beloved by accountants in the presence of non-financial managers, simply means that the item in question is deemed to be worth nothing, so its cost is to be written off as an expense somewhere in the P&L Account, that is, deducted from profit.)

A typical calculation looks like this:

	Opening balance	240,212
add:	Purchases	88,609
	Available for use	328,821
less:	Closing stock	212,604
	Cost of sales	116,217 (stock used)

2 *Labour* can be taken as the actual wages incurred by the production departments in making the products for sale. Technically, there will be a timing difference between the products being made and those being sold, since the finished items go into stock first. Accountants can adjust this by allowing for increases or falls in the stock level, but if production and sales quantities are relatively similar, the timing difference is insignificant. It is permissible for part of the labour cost to be included in the valuation of the stock, so it is not deducted from the profit until that stock is sold. The logic is that it costs money to use labour to transform raw materials into work in progress and finished goods, so the value should reflect that. Direct costs can also be incorporated into the stock value, for the same reason.

3 *Direct costs* are basically production overheads, and the actual costs incurred can be used. This will include such expenses as electricity, perhaps a share of the rates bill, depreciation of factory plant and machinery. In theory if there was no

production, there would be nil direct production costs, which is a pretty useful definition of what a direct production cost is. This doesn't hold for the rates charge (it's a fixed cost for the year), but most companies would include it anyway, since a factory is the major reason for the rates bill being the size that it is.

The cost of making a single unit of the product can be given a theoretical cost for each element of material, labour and direct overhead. The cost of sales in the P&L Account is then the sold quantity multiplied by these costs per unit. This figure can then be amended up or down by any variances in manufacturing performance between the expected standards and actual.

Gross profit – is simply the difference between the sales and the cost of sales. However, it can be read as a simple measure of the profitability of making or supplying the product to customers, before taking into consideration indirect and fixed costs.

Overheads – covers costs and expenses which are not directly associated with the production of the goods, but include all the necessary support functions needed to run the company. In our example the overheads have been broken down into staff costs, depreciation and indirect costs. There is no doubt that the management would have access to a more detailed analysis of the figures that lay behind these costs. The analysis may be by department and would certainly, in the case of indirect overhead costs, go down to the level of recording the type of cost, e.g. stationery, equipment hire, legal fees, bank charges, etc. Senior management may not want to know what the stationery bill for the period is, but somebody somewhere in the organization ought to know. Otherwise how could the cost of anything be monitored and controlled?

The **staff costs** will relate to the salaries/wages, pension and National Insurance contributions of the company for employees not directly related to production (i.e. those not included in the labour figure under cost of sales). So the wage costs of Sales and Marketing, Human Resources, Management, Administration, IT, R&D and even Accounts will be included.

Depreciation – this is such a commonly misunderstood term that a full explanation is merited at this point. The concept stems from how the profits should be affected if a company buys an expensive piece of capital equipment or an equally costly building. If the company's annual profits are say £8m, and a new milling machine costs £2m, how does this affect the reported profit?

The argument for using depreciation runs along these lines:

* given that the company is performing consistently, we would expect to see a consistent result in the reported profits of the company
* the milling machine will last for ten years
* to report suddenly only a £6m profit would make the management appear, at first glance, to be less effective than they really had been
* so, if the machine will last for ten years, let's give a tenth of the cost of it to each of these years and reduce the profit accordingly – by £200,000 for each year, rather than by £2m in a single year.

The depreciation is the amount deducted from profits by dividing the original cost of the capital item by how long it should last (technically, its economic life). This is called the *straight line method* and is the most popular.

The *reducing balance method* calculates depreciation as a percentage of the closing net book value, e.g. if the depreciation is set at 10% p.a. and the original cost was £10,000:

Original cost	£10,000
Year 1 depreciation	(£1,000)
Net book value	£9,000
Year 2 depreciation	(£900)
Net book value	£8,100
Year 3 depreciation	£810
Net book value	£7,390 and so on.

It takes longer to fully depreciate the asset than it would using the straight line method over ten years.

Note that the depreciation amount is not affected by when the item is paid for – it could be paid for by cash on delivery, 30 days' credit, a seven-year lease contract, or whatever. Cash has nothing to do with depreciation and vice versa. Depreciation is purely an accounting adjustment to spread the cost of the item over a number of years rather than take a big reduction in the profits of one year. The company does not literally put aside cash to pay for a new one when the old one is obsolete (see also *fixed assets*).

Profit before interest and tax (PBIT) – is simply a subtotal, although this is most often the line on the P&L Account which managers accept as being the best measure of their performance. Subsequent additional reductions in this profit figure, namely interest and tax, could be considered beyond the control of most of the managers involved in operational activities, so this is why they tend to think of PBIT, and sometimes refer to it, as the 'bottom line'. To be more accurate, the real 'bottom line' is literally the last line on the published P&L Account, after all deductions for interest, tax and dividends have been made, but the PBIT does for most managers.

Interest – is a common enough concept, and fortunate is the company that receives more than it pays. Such a company may have good cash management, or just be in the sort of business that encourages a build up of cash (e.g. retail outlets, which get paid in cash (or near cash) by customers, but have their supplies on credit terms).

Normally, interest payable is a straightforward deduction from the profit, except in those cases where a company decides to capitalize some interest as being part of a fixed asset project that required loans to carry it out. Of course this means less interest is deducted from the profit, so the profit is higher, which is generally a nice thing for managers to see! Note that it is the true 'bottom line' – the profit after interest, tax and dividends – which is carried over to the Balance Sheet as this year's profit.

The P&L Account in the statutory accounts

The statutory accounts are accessible to the public (and other companies or their accountants) via Companies House, so companies generally try to report the minimum possible. There will be far less detail in the statutory format than in the management accounts, although there will be some explanatory notes. A typical Profit and Loss Account in the statutory accounts may look as simple as this:

	Notes	Year ended 30.06.11 £000	Year ended 30.06.10 £000
Io Exploration Limited			
Profit and Loss Account			
for the twelve months ended 30 June 2011			
Turnover	1		
– continuing operations		892	832
Cost of sales		612	574
Gross profit		280	258
Other operating expenses	2	204	196
Profit on ordinary activities before interest		76	62
Interest payable		44	56
Profit on ordinary activities before taxation		32	6
Tax		6	1
Profit on ordinary activities after taxation		26	5

Even the explanatory notes 1 and 2 do not give a lot away: there will be details of sales by region, specific deductions from profit (such as depreciation, the audit fee and operating rentals) and perhaps, most interestingly, an indication of payments to directors. Individuals are not named specifically and the note will appear like this:

| Emoluments of highest-paid director | £84,200 |
| Emoluments of other directors: | |

	No. of directors
£0 – £5,000	2
£50,001 – £60,000	1
£60,001 – £70,000	1

The two directors paid below £5,000 are likely to be non-executive directors, who have an advisory role rather than daily participation in the running of the company.

The balance sheet

Another major report is the Balance Sheet. The Balance Sheet indicates at how much the business is valued. Very importantly, this value is taken at the end of the accounting period. It is only a snapshot of the business at a specific date, which means that the day after, the figures on the Balance Sheet can (indeed, will) change. It isn't likely to be a material difference, at least not for the first few days or weeks.

However, since the management are aware that the Balance Sheet at the year end will be the one publicly available, they are usually sensible enough to make it look as good as possible, perhaps by some short-term manipulations of key figures, such as cash, by delaying payment to suppliers.

Given that limited companies have nine months after their financial year end to file their results at Companies House, the Balance Sheet data can be quite out of date by the time it is publicly available. Don't assume that the values in the Balance Sheet apply to the company months later, or even that the figures are in similar ratios to each other, particularly with companies operating in industries with seasonal variations in trading levels.

There are three major areas in a Balance Sheet – assets, liabilities and equity.

* *Assets* – are items either owned by the company, owed to it or something in which it has a beneficial interest.
* *Liabilities* – are items that the company owes to others, usually debts of one form or another.
* *Equity* – is deemed to be the amounts due to the owners of the company, the shareholders. It includes the profits of the company.

As a matter of course, the Balance Sheet will always balance (naturally) and all the assets will equal the sum of the liabilities and the equity. It cannot be any other way.

The following terms make up the sections to be found on most balance sheets.

Fixed assets

Fixed assets are items acquired by the company that are not quickly consumed during the course of their use. Definitions vary from one organization to another, but most companies have authorization procedures for the acquisition of fixed assets, usually under the name of capital expenditure. A common definition is any tangible items costing £1,000 or more which will last for more than a year, although the amount does vary in different companies.

The alternative to treating a cost as a fixed asset is to expense it – deduct it from the profits in the accounting period it was acquired. There are grey areas in the definition of fixed assets because, when the principle was established, the idea was that you had just bought a hulking great machine, something for all to see. So it would be all right to capitalize (meaning treat as a fixed asset) an expensive computer; but what about the equally expensive software? Is it tangible? You can't touch the programs, but the computer is no good without them. Some companies do capitalize software and some don't.

So would you consider any of the following to be fixed assets:

* maintenance costs on repairing a dockyard crane?
* spending £2,000 on replacing the motor of a conveyor belt?
* the architect's fees for drawing up the plans of a new office block?

The answers are no, yes (with a condition) and yes.

* The first is deemed to be a running cost (i.e. deducted from profit), because it is the nature of maintenance repairs to be done periodically, several times a year.
* The motor replacement can be added to the fixed asset register (simply a list of fixed assets acquired), but the original motor must be deducted, scrapped off.
* Architect's fees defy the definition of tangibility, but the building wouldn't proceed without the plans, so they are included. The rules aren't necessarily hard and fast – there is often considerable scope for interpretation and artistic licence!

Fixed assets are typically divided into such categories as land and buildings, plant and machinery, fixtures and fittings, and vehicles. In essence, they are items of a tangible nature that are too expensive to be deducted from the profit in the year in which they were acquired. Instead the cost of them is spread over an arbitrary lifespan given to each category (say ten years for plant and machinery), through the depreciation charge to the Profit and Loss Account.

The 'life' of the asset is, in theory, supposed to be its economic life, or how long it will last. However, this judgement is left to the directors and the easiest way to do it is to group assets together in the above categories and depreciate each category at a given rate. The usual sort of lifespans and annual depreciation rates you will encounter are:

Land	**nil (it doesn't wear out)**
Buildings	**20 to 60 years (5% to 1.67%)**
Plant and machinery	**5 to 10 years (20% to 10%)**
Fixtures and fittings	**5 to 10 years (20% to 10%)**
Vehicles	**3 to 5 years (33% to 20%)**

Of course, when the asset is fully depreciated (that is when the accumulated depreciation over the years equals the original cost of the asset and it is said to be fully written off), it does not mean that the item is no longer usable. There's many a twenty-year-old machine working away quite happily although, according to the books of the company, it has no value!

This actually caused a problem to accountants, because they felt that it meant they were understating the value of their assets on the Balance Sheet. Resourceful as ever, a new accounting rule was developed which allowed the assets to be revalued, at a figure to be determined by the directors. Of course, the auditors would require some justification for a twenty-year-old machine with a nil book value suddenly appearing on the books at £50,000, but there are professional valuers who will calculate a 'proper' value (for a fee).

A few common definitions to finish off fixed assets:

Gross book value (GBV) – is the original (historic) cost of the asset, or the revaluation amount, if it has one.

Accumulated depreciation – is the sum of the depreciation charged to the Profit and Loss Account over the years. It may be shown as:

Accumulated depreciation brought forward	£220,000
Depreciation charged to profit this year	£74,000
Accumulated depreciation carried forward	£294,000

The figure for the depreciation charged this year is the same as appears in the Profit and Loss Account under, naturally, depreciation. This is also used in the Cash Flow Statement, added back to the reconciliation because depreciation is not a cash item.

Net book value (NBV) – is the difference between the gross book value and the accumulated depreciation and is the value given to the asset in the company's accounts.

Profit/loss on disposal – is the difference between the proceeds received for a sold asset and its net book value, and appears in the P&L Account.

So for a fork lift truck costing £15,000 three years ago, depreciated over five years (at 20% depreciation p.a.) and sold for £8,000, the profit made on the disposal is:

Gross book value	£15,000
Accumulated depreciation	£9,000 (3 @ £3,000 p.a.)
Net book value	£6,000
Proceeds on sale	£8,000
Profit on disposal	£2,000

Revaluation reserve – is a section in the equity part of the Balance Sheet. This is the balancing entry to the increase in the value of the fixed assets following a revaluation exercise. By law, the directors cannot take this amount into consideration when calculating how much of the equity can be given to the shareholders as a dividend. It is a form of 'non-distributable reserve'. Only trading profits are distributable.

Leased assets – are items of a capital nature that have not been purchased outright, but have been leased from a finance company. There is, in essence, a loan from the finance company (the lessor) in order to acquire the particular asset. Interest is built into the repayments, which reduce the capital borrowed much like a repayment mortgage. At the end of the lease, all payments having been made, the title (ownership) of the asset passes to the company from the lessor.

The hire purchase or contract hire of an item is different in that ownership or title always stays with the finance company and, at the end of the contract period, the asset is handed back to the finance company (or a mere peppercorn rent paid for its continued use). Given that title will never pass to the company, the asset is excluded from the Balance Sheet – and so is the liability to pay the finance company. This is why such schemes are known as 'off balance sheet financing'. They are, however, usually declared in a note to the accounts as 'operating leases/rentals', with a summary of the amounts the company is obliged to pay in the next year, between two to five years, and beyond five years.

Goodwill – is an intangible concept of an asset. It is an accounting adjustment which basically reflects the difference between the amount a company pays to acquire another company and the book value of the assets of the purchased company as shown in its accounts.

Asset value of purchased company	£4,500,000
Consideration paid	£5,200,000
Goodwill on acquisition	£700,000

Why would you pay more for a company than its own accounts suggest it is worth? There are all sorts of strategic and commercial reasons:

* brand name
* geographic base
* customer list
* complementary products
* security of key supplies
* potential synergies
* patents and licences
* R&D technology
* management skills.

Goodwill is created by many things, but it is essentially a question of perception. A company's books (accounts) say that it is worth one value, but an acquiring company values it differently. Goodwill can be depreciated like a normal fixed asset, although suggested practice is now to write off the goodwill (and reduce the profits in the year) when the company is bought.

Current assets

Current assets are different from fixed assets in that they actually change quite quickly. Stock is purchased from a supplier on credit, and sold to a customer who becomes a debtor. The customer pays, the payment is banked and the creditor paid. This cycle can take from a few days to several months, depending upon the nature of the business (compare a bakery to a building company).

The items included in the definition of current assets are:

Cash – how much money the organization has. This will actually differ from the current bank balance due to payments which have been lodged at the bank but that have not yet cleared the account, and issued cheques not having been processed, just like a personal account. The figure shown in the Balance Sheet is always the cash book figure, not the bank balance.

Cash is one of the key figures people tend to focus upon, quite rightly. It follows, therefore, that the management, in order to impress, may attempt to ensure that the cash balance at the year end is a respectable one. Remember, the Balance Sheet shows the position of the company on a *particular day* at the end of its financial year. To achieve this, managers may delay payments to suppliers in the last few weeks of the financial year to protect the cash position.

Most people know that this goes on and that, in the first few days of the new financial year, the cash goes flying out to appease the patient creditors. It would be more useful for a company to report its average monthly cash balance as a note to the accounts. This would give a better indication of the management's cash handling abilities, but as things stand, the closing cash position is all you get.

Trade debtors – how much the organization is owed by its customers, which comes from sales invoices less credit notes and money received. This includes the VAT charged on invoices, since the customers must pay this in order for the company to pass it on to HM Revenue and Customs.

Prepayments – how much the organization has paid in advance for goods and services. Normally this is a relatively small amount, but think of things like insurance or rates. The bill for the following twelve months may have to be paid all at once, but the cost of it will be spread over the year.

Stocks – also known as inventory. This is the value, at the lowest of cost or net realizable value, of the items that the company sells. The reason for the alternative method of valuing stocks is that, if the company possesses some obsolete stock that no one will buy (like Betamax video recorders), they should be valued at how much they could be sold for rather than what they cost.

Current liabilities

These are the debts of the company, payable in the relatively short term, a year or less.

Trade creditors – how much is owed to suppliers of goods and services. Some of this will have already been invoiced, but even if it has not, provision must be made with an 'accrual' in anticipation of the invoice. This relates back to the concept of matching the timing of recording costs to when they were incurred rather than waiting for an invoice. As with debtors, the amounts in creditors include VAT charged by suppliers on their invoices. This input VAT can be deducted from the output VAT added to sales to form the net amount due to HM Revenue and Customs.

Other creditors – how much is owed to other parties, such as value added tax (VAT), income tax (PAYE), national insurance contributions (NIC), employees (if paid a week or month in hand), sundry accruals, etc.

Working capital

This term is usually the sum of the current assets less the current liabilities, although some companies do not include cash in the calculation. In theory, if the number comes out as negative, i.e. the organization's current liabilities are greater than its current assets, then the organization is in a risky position. Even if it could turn all its assets into cash, there would not be enough to meet all its liabilities. However, this is only a very general rule, since much depends on the nature of the assets and liabilities, the timing of the reports and, indeed, the type of industry.

Net assets

Sometimes called capital employed, this is simply the sum of the fixed assets and the working capital (including cash). This figure is also used in ratio calculations, principally in working out the rate of return on capital employed (ROCE).

Long-term liabilities

The distinction between these and current liabilities is that long-term liabilities are not due for at least a year. Consequently, it will include items such as loans (but a bank overdraft would be classified as a current liability, since they are usually repayable on demand) and the amounts outstanding (obligations) on assets which have been leased rather than bought.

Equity

In theory, this is what is 'owed' to the shareholders or owners of the organization. It can comprise:

Capital – the initial and subsequent investments by the owners, the shareholders. These are proceeds from issues of shares in the company. This definition of capital is not to be confused with capital expenditure on fixed assets. This means a company can issue shares perhaps to finance the building and equipping of a new factory, or to raise capital to buy capital assets!

The reward for investing in a company is given to shareholders in the form of a dividend payment, but only if there are sufficient profits for the directors of the company to deem such a payment advisable. Of course, if they go too long paying small dividends or none at all, the shareholders may prefer to have new directors running the company!

Reserves – there are different types, the most common of which are:

* **Retained profits**, being the sum of all the profits made historically, less any dividends paid out. In theory, this is what the shareholders are entitled to take out of the company as dividends and it can be split into several categories as shown below:

Retained profits brought forward	£16,852,200
Profit this year	£2,654,600
Dividends	(£1,400,000)
Retained profits carried forward	£18,106,800

The profit for the year comes directly from the Profit and Loss Account – it is the profit after interest and tax have been deducted, but obviously before dividends (otherwise these would be deducted twice).

* **Revaluation reserve**, made when the fixed assets are restated in the accounts at a higher value than they were previously shown. Since this is just a notional accounting increase in the value of the assets and is not backed up by real money (remember this is merely someone's opinion of the value of the assets and nobody has actually bought them at that price), this cannot be taken into account when the directors come to consider how much dividend to pay out.

Preference shares – are something of a hybrid between equity and debt. They are a certain type of share in the company which allows the holder to receive interest on the investment before the holder of ordinary shares is entitled to receive a dividend. But payment is not compulsory, like it is for interest on loans. With cumulative preference shares, however, if the company does skip a payment due to lack of sufficient profits or cash, the deficit can be carried forward until it is eventually made up.

Notes to the accounts pertaining to the Balance Sheet give some analysis of the summary amounts reported in the Balance Sheet itself. Long-term creditors may be analysed by how many years ahead the amounts are due to be paid.

Intercompany debtors and creditors

Companies in the same group (with the same ultimate parent holding company) may trade with each other. Instead of showing their respective accounts in trade debtors and creditors, they are isolated as intercompany debtors and creditors. These can perhaps be taken as a measure of how much support a company gets from others in its group, particularly from its parent company if that is a substantial creditor.

Intercompany debtors and creditors appear under current assets and liabilities respectively, again because they are perceived as being settled on demand (or following an instruction from head office!).

When the accounts of the member companies are consolidated, all the intercompany balances should net out to zero and disappear.

A = L + E

Note that in the Balance Sheet, total assets always equals total liabilities plus equity. This can also be presented as total assets less total liabilities equals equity, being mathematically a rearrangement of the same equation.

The cash flow statement

We have already established that cash is a critical factor of success to any enterprise. Profits are all very well, but a business must have cash in order to survive. The two are not necessarily automatically complementary, but both are needed for the long-term good of the firm.

The cash flow cycle

Cash comes in from customers from sales made and goes out of the business to pay suppliers for goods and services. Since such transactions are not settled immediately, there is the interim stage of debtors and creditors.

Consider the flow of cash if Lidd Enterprises, a wholesaler in laser printers, acquires ten printers at £300 each from the manufacturers at the start of January, to be paid for in four weeks time. Just two weeks later, it sells all ten at £450 each to a valued customer, who will pay in a further four weeks.

Upon receipt from the supplier the printers go into stock, while at the same time Lidd has a creditor (the supplier). When they are sold, they move out of stock as Lidd acquires a debtor (the customer). At the end of January, cash goes out to pay the creditor, then in mid-February (28 days after the sale) comes in from the debtor. The cycle looks like this:

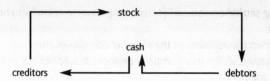

It is apparent that cash in the operating cycle either comes from debtors or goes out to creditors. Stock in itself does not create a cash movement. An increase in stock levels means higher creditors, until they are paid. A fall in stock levels gives a rise in debtors, who will eventually pay.

Non-cash items

So what causes the difference between profits and cash? In an earlier example, we looked at the timing issues involved when suppliers have to be paid before customers pay up, leading to a net outflow of cash in the short term. Over a longer period, because the amounts being received from customers are greater than those being paid out to suppliers, cash will begin to accumulate.

But when we consider the accounting profits of a company, we are dealing with a different subject. Within those neat columns of numbers, headed by £ signs, are a number of items which affect the profit, but have nothing to do with cash at all! The most significant one is usually depreciation. As previously explained, this is an accounting convention to spread the cost of a fixed asset over more than one year. Considering the size of some items of capital expenditure (e.g. a power station), this is perfectly understandable. Even so, paying for a piece of machinery for the factory costing £100,000, which is depreciated over ten years, will only deduct £10,000 from the year's profits, but the full £100,000 from the bank account when it is paid for!

By the same token, the following year, a further £10,000 depreciation will be deducted from profit, but with nil effect on the cash position – it was all paid for in the previous year.

Similarly, the profit or loss made on the disposal of fixed assets is not a cash item. The actual proceeds received from the sale are, but the profit/loss includes the net book value of the asset at the time it was sold, after years of depreciation have been set against it. Consider a computer bought for £10,000 depreciated over five years:

Year	1	2	3	4
Cost (£)	10,000			
Depreciation (£)	2,000	2,000	2,000	2,000
Net book value (£)	8,000	6,000	4,000	2,000
Proceeds on sale (£)				3,500
Profit on disposal (£)				1,500

The depreciation is a deduction from profit each year.
Contrast the cash flows in the four years:

Year	1	2	3	4
Purchase (£)	(10,000)			
Sale (£)				3,500

A simple way of looking at cash

In its published accounts, a company will show how much it had in its cash book (the cash in the bank or the overdraft figure) at the end of its financial year and one year earlier as a comparison. It is simple to tell if it has more or less cash than it did last year.

This can be too simplistic a way of looking at the cash flow, but it generally gives a pretty good guide. It does not automatically reveal if there were loans taken out or new capital raised to bring in more cash, nor does it indicate what money was spent on. The Cash Flow Statement gives a better indication of those events.

The formal Cash Flow Statement

Under the current rules, the Cash Flow Statement that appears as part of the company's published accounts must be analysed as five component parts:

1 Net cash flow from operating activities
2 Returns on investment and servicing of finance

3 Taxation

4 Investing activities

5 Financing.

The five parts are added up to give an increase or decrease in cash and cash equivalent. The final format would look like this:

Cash Flow Statement for year ended 30 September 2009	£000	£000
Net cash inflow from operating activities		2,440
Returns on investments and servicing of finance		
Interest received	44	
Interest paid	(212)	
Dividends paid	(850)	
Net cash inflow from returns on investments and servicing of finance		(1,018)
Taxation		
Corporation tax paid	(331)	
Tax paid		(331)
Investing activities		
Payments for tangible fixed assets	(102)	
Receipts from sales of tangible fixed assets	27	
Net cash outflow from investing activities		(75)
Net cash inflow before financing		1,016
Financing		–
Increase in cash and cash equivalents		1,016

Notes to the accounts will add a little analysis to some of the figures in the Cash Flow Statement, but all the figures in the statement are taken from the Profit and Loss Account or the Balance Sheet.

The Cash Flow Statement really explains where the money has come from and gone to. It starts with the net cash inflow from operating activities, which is initially the operating profit (before taxation, interest and dividends) adjusted for any non-cash items used to reach that profit, such as depreciation. This is further adjusted by the movement in the items of working capital over the year. The changes in stock, debtors and creditors are deemed to be consumers or creators of cash, depending upon the direction in which they have moved.

An increase in stocks or debtors is deemed to reduce cash, as does a decrease in creditors (they're being paid). And vice versa for all three. A stock increase does not literally decrease cash, it would normally cause creditors to rise, but if there is not a corresponding match, then the implication is that the stock has been paid for, therefore cash has gone out of the company to the creditors.

The returns on investments and servicing of finance is a long way of saying dividends and interest, paid and received. Taxation refers only to corporation tax, although advance corporation tax, which is triggered by the payment of dividends, is included. VAT is not, since it is included in the creditors figure. Investing activities covers the purchase and sale of fixed assets. Finally, financing identifies further influxes of cash from shareholders through share issues and any long-term loans taken out or repaid.

Points of interest

The way to interpret the cash flow of a company is to ask a few key questions and determine the answers from the stated figures.

Firstly, has the cash at the bank increased or otherwise? Decreases are not usually a good sign, unless the company has spent on something that appears to have profit potential, such as acquiring another company, or building another factory. However, an increase may be brought about by good cash flow management – or perhaps by taking out a loan, in order to pay for a proposed expansion. The answers have to be looked for, but they can be found.

A good place to start is the working capital. Very broadly speaking, assuming that trading conditions have not radically altered, stocks, debtors and creditors ought to be roughly in line with sales, comparing year to year. If debtors have risen relatively, it may, just may, suggest that longer credit terms have been offered to customers to secure sales. If creditors have gone up too, then they are the ones who are paying for it!

Then look at fixed asset purchases. Is money being spent on the future of the company? Is it as much as last year, bearing in mind that some investments in assets may occur only every twenty years or more, such as building a new factory for increased production capacity?

There's not much that can be done about tax and interest payments, although tax planning can minimize the former. The only way to pay less interest is to owe less.

Which leads nicely to looking at the movement in loans, whether they have increased or fallen; similarly with issues of capital to raise money from shareholders. Injections of large amounts of cash can be required by a company for two reasons – to finance an expansion of one sort or another which is so large that current cash amounts are insufficient to finance it; or to keep the creditors at bay so they don't have the company bankrupted and wound up out of existence. Interpret the Profit and Loss Account, the Balance Sheet and the Cash Flow Statement to decide which way it is.

4

audit of annual accounts

If it can be said that managers don't care for accountants, then accountants don't always go out of their way to welcome auditors. Strange, because auditors are accountants too. Their task is not to draw up the financial information, that's what the accountants in the company do. No, what the auditors do is to check that it's right, as best they can, in a short space of time. It's a legal requirement for limited companies and plcs, so this is a quick look at how they go about verifying their accounting brethren are doing their jobs properly.

Who is an auditor?

Auditors are accountants too. As members of the Institute of Chartered Accountants in England and Wales (ICAEW), the Institute of Chartered Accountants in Scotland, or the Irish Institute, they are the only people allowed, by company law, to audit the accounts of limited companies.

The accounts for a company are prepared by the accountants who are employed by it. They are usually qualified themselves, perhaps with the ICAEW or one of the other professional bodies. So surely the accounts will be all right – there's no need to have them audited, is there?

In the vast majority of cases, there are no problems. The auditor confirms the figures prepared by the company, adds a statement to the accounts to that effect and then moves on to his next audit.

The need for an audit

There was a time when auditors weren't needed. Many years ago, most organizations were run by the people who had put up the money to start with. As commerce and trade expanded, large amounts of capital were required to put expensive machines in big buildings and businesses became too big for the owners to run by themselves. This meant that the investors were not necessarily also the managers of the company.

Now that in itself was not a problem. Except that the managers were responsible for reporting what the profits of the company were to the owners and when there was not sufficient profit made to pay a dividend to the owners, the owners wanted proof that this was the case. The owners may have become a mite suspicious, especially when the managing director started driving a new-fangled Henry Ford machine.

So an independent authority was established and company law passed so that all companies that had limited liability to their creditors (instead of unlimited personal liability of the owners or managers) had to have their annual accounts audited. This validation and verification could only be done by suitably qualified people – chartered accountants.

An audit in practice

What actually happens in an audit is that the company's accountant prepares the figures, as agreed by the board of directors (who bear ultimate responsibility for the figures – they literally have to sign them before they are sent to Companies House). The auditors then arrive and begin to check the numbers.

Now if a company reports sales of £15,252,368, the auditors do not go through all the invoices and credit notes issued that year and add them all up to verify the total. Instead they do sample checks, picking out a few (generally high value) invoices and asking to see proofs of delivery and that the customer has paid the invoice (unless it is still showing in the debtors ledger).

The auditors issue circulation letters to the top few debtors and creditors, asking them to confirm the balances that the company is showing in its year end accounts. After all, stating in the accounts that British Airways owes the company £3,000,000 might make a significant contribution to the assets of the company – but if British Airways only agrees to owing £400,000, something's wrong somewhere.

So that is the approach of the auditors – to see if something might be wrong. They have only a limited time in which to complete the audit, possibly as little as a week for a company with a turnover of less than £5m. Another problem the auditors face is that they usually have very limited knowledge of the systems of the company they are checking. Different companies have different computers, different procedures, and the auditors have to fathom these out during their short time there.

Rules of engagement

Fortunately for the auditors, they are not required to get all 'i's dotted and 't's crossed. They use a concept of materiality.

So what if a credit note for £1,500 missed the cut off at the end of the financial year? If sales are £10m, then the amount of the credit note is neither here nor there. It's not significant enough to have the accounts changed – it is immaterial.

One of the rules that auditors must follow is to ensure that the accounts are *prudent* and *conservative* in their reporting of profitability. This means, if the auditor is in any doubt, the profits should be understated so as not to mislead current and prospective investors as to the merits of the organization. So they check that stock is not overvalued (by comparing prices paid for the items with their unit value in stock) and how currency exchange differences are included or otherwise in profit, among other things.

The auditors will also be looking for consistency in the way the figures have been prepared. Given that some of the rules for accountancy are somewhat flexible, it is important that those who want to use the company's accounts can compare like with like. So if the company depreciated plant and machinery over five years last year, it ought to do the same this year. The management cannot suddenly decide that because profits are a bit on the low side, a ten-year depreciation policy would improve the results. Certainly, if they did change the depreciation policy, the auditors would want a better explanation.

At the very least, if there is a change in any accounting policy, it has to be declared in a note to the accounts for the first year of change. This does reveal to the alert reader of the accounts that something is afoot.

Relationship between auditors and management

The auditors are utterly independent of the company and its management. But they are paid by the company to carry out the audit. Some uncharitable minds might suggest that this puts the auditors in a difficult situation. After all, although the directors are obliged by law to appoint auditors to make the independent checks, there is no obligation on the company to keep the same audit firm year in and year out. So does this mean, if the auditors find something they are not happy with, they simply ignore it for fear of upsetting the directors and losing a lucrative fee? (Some audit fees for major plcs run into millions of pounds. But note that the cost of the audit is always isolated in the notes to the accounts.)

No, of course not. The upper hand is with the auditors, for two reasons.

1 If the auditors are insistent that the accounts, as they stand, are not correct, they can refuse to sign them off (approve them as being accurate) or give them only qualified approval. That tells readers of the accounts that there's something odd, but that the auditors and the management couldn't agree on who was right. At the very best, this is a disastrous piece of public relations for the company, since outsiders will wonder what is going on with the company's financial reporting.

2 The directors are entitled to appoint new auditors. However, the replacement auditors will be highly suspicious of why their predecessors were removed – it's an uncommon thing for auditors to be changed. They will be on their guard immediately for any signs of wrongdoing.

There are grey areas in accounting, such as brand valuation, where the management may feel that it is right and want to stick to its guns. The auditors may simply possess a different opinion, but if it is one they are strongly convinced of, the accounts will not get full approval.

A company can keep the same auditors for years and it is this cosy relationship that bothers some people. There is a suggestion, which may come into legal force eventually, that companies should be compelled to change their auditors every three years or less. This would prevent audit firms from being overreliant on next year's audit fee – and if they're going to lose the business anyway, they might as well be as forthright as necessary. But it could just become a game of musical auditors, with auditors swapping companies.

Appointing new auditors is a simple task, done at the annual general meeting. In an agenda for such a meeting, there is usually a resolution to re-appoint the current auditors for the next year, at a remuneration to be determined by the directors, or to appoint new ones.

The stamp of approval

So, if everything has gone well, the accounts will be published and filed at Companies House for all to see. In the accounts there is a page signed by the auditors, declaring the accounts to be, in their opinion, a 'true and fair view' of the financial state of the company.

So that means – what? A true view? There is no definition in company law of what a true view is or, for that matter, a fair one. So does true mean accurate or correct? We already know that auditors operate with a level of materiality, so the numbers don't have to be spot on. It's more likely that 'true' is used to mean 'true as opposed to false'.

'Fair' is a little harder to understand. It seems to imply that the numbers probably, in the opinion of the auditors, give a pretty reasonable idea of what's gone on in the company over the past year. It's all a bit vague really.

Still, if the accounts have been signed off by the auditors, surely they must be right? Not according to the auditors.

There has been a legal case in which investors relied on the audited accounts when making their decision to put money into the company. Unfortunately, it turned out that there must have been something wrong somewhere, because they lost their money. Naturally, they blamed the auditors for producing a report that, they felt, was utter rubbish. Not our fault you lost your money, claimed the auditors. For one thing, it now appears that the directors of the company didn't tell us everything that was going on – if they had, we wouldn't have approved the accounts. Furthermore, they suggested, you shouldn't use the accounts as a basis for investment.

This was a major denial of the auditors' responsibility – what use are published accounts if even the auditors say you can't actually rely upon them? The claims of the auditors were understandable. If they had agreed liability, it would have set a very expensive precedent leading to claims for damages by investors who felt they had been misled by information in approved accounts.

But the courts agreed that the auditors did owe a duty of care to readers of the accounts and that they cannot just wash their hands of the whole thing. However, the investors' case was weakened because they ought to have taken other financial information (presumably historic records, performances of competitors and the industry) into account – the accounts of the company should have formed only a part of their knowledge before deciding to invest.

The credibility of audited accounts, and auditors in particular, took a heavy knock in this sad episode. It's a pity really, because the vast majority of accounts are probably perfectly all right, but the media aren't interested in those cases.

5

financial information for managers

If there is one book that managers new to heading up a department or section ought to be given, it might be a good suggestion to make it this one. And if they could only have one chapter out of that book, this ought to be it. Sadly, few managers get any financial training, and the first they know of the management information pack, with its sales and margin analysis, customer and product profitability, overheads statements, cash flow forecasts, numerous ratios, backed up by sundry reports of obsolete stock items and overdue debtor, is when they get it. If only, like you, they had read this chapter.

Saving up for rainy days

It could be said that there are more than one set of financial results for a company. The first is the one the accountant prepares to establish the numbers she's happy with. This can be adjusted to allow for any discrepancies that may come to light later on, just in case something has been missed. The accountant's version forms the results given to the managing director. He may think that the results are awfully good this month, so why not squirrel some of it away in case next month isn't so good? A couple more simple journals could provide for some potential costs to reduce the profits nicely.

When it comes to the financial year end, all those bits either have to be put back into the accounts or explained to the auditors (assuming the auditors find them). This will be the basis of the 'real' results but the management may want to move the profit up or down. This may be to show steady, rather than exceptional, growth against last year, in case the shareholders expect the same again next year or to bring taxable losses forward. Knowing that customers and competitors will see the results can also make a difference (would you be happy if a supplier was making very large profits?). They might do a little extra writing off of stock, fixed assets or bad debtors, or try to have stock revalued a little higher. Generally it is easier to lose some of the profit than add to it.

Financial v. management accounts

The three major financial accounts are available for anyone to examine. They also leave many questions unanswered.

The management accounts, on the other hand, have a restricted circulation because they are much more detailed. The management accounts are usually more than just a set of accounts – it is frequently a whole pack of financial information, often accompanied by non-financial data such as head counts, production quantities and commentaries from various managers explaining what has happened in the period and why.

This pack tends to be very focused on the profit and loss side of operations, rather than the Balance Sheet. This is because most non-financial managers feel they understand sales and costs better than things like debtors, creditors, lease obligations and other Balance Sheet items and that sales and costs are under their control, while those Balance Sheet lines are the responsibility of the Accounts department.

The first point can be overcome by education (such as reading a good book on the subject!). The second point is understandable when you consider that the Accounts department is responsible for collecting money and paying it out. However, when enlightenment comes, these managers will realize that the sources of debtors and creditors are sales and purchases respectively, and these are not Accounts functions! The level of creditors to be paid depends upon the purchases made and most managers make purchases of one sort or another. The fewer purchases made, the less stock and fewer creditors there are, with less demand on cash to pay them.

Contents of the management accounts pack

The key document is the Profit and Loss Account, or it may be referred to as an Income or Operating Statement. Like the P&L Account in the financial accounts, it will start with sales, although there may be some simple analysis such as home/export or own sales/factored. Then comes the cost of sales, deducted from sales to give a gross margin.

Overheads in management accounts are usually reported at departmental level, whereas they can be summarized in financial accounts. Department heads are responsible for the expenditure within their departments and so need to know what the actual results are, preferably against budget.

Deducting overheads from gross margin produces an operating profit. Depreciation may be charged as a single figure or allocated to departments (in line with their use of fixed assets), depending upon the company's (or accountant's) philosophy. Often this is as 'low' as management accounts go. Although the financial accounts have more lines, with deductions for interest and tax, management accounts are for the use of managers in their daily operational activities. Interest and taxation rates are generally beyond their control, although hopefully not their understanding.

The rest of the pack

In no particular order, the rest of the management accounts may include the following financial information.

Sales and margin analysis

This breaks down the sales and margin for the month, usually by customer, as shown below.

	£
Norrison	212,020
B&B	70,412
Ohio Stores	44,885
Spanners	22,694
Doricos	18,936
Tristram	15,220
Other	40,650
Total	424,817

The analysis could be by customer category or type (DIY centre, superstore, etc.) if that would be more useful to the management, or even by product (individual, range or group).

Alongside the sales figure, the gross margin can also be shown – if it is known of course (it could be derived from the costing system, actual or standard). It is certainly a useful thing to be aware of – compare this table with the previous one which had sales only:

	Sales (£)	Margin (£)	%
Norrison	212,020	50,650	23.8
B&B	70,412	24,298	34.5
Ohio Stores	44,885	21,640	48.2
Spanners	22,694	11,395	50.2
Doricos	18,936	7,222	38.1
Tristram	15,220	2,350	15.4
Other	40,650	14,612	35.9
Total	424,817	132,167	31.2

Suddenly doing business with Norrison doesn't seem that great. Perhaps more emphasis should be placed on increasing sales to Ohio and Spanners, and maybe Tristram should be dropped altogether – after taking into consideration selling and distribution costs, this business may run at a loss.

Before jumping to such conclusions though, more information is needed. This is only one month's results and it may not be a fair reflection of the normal sales and margin. Adding a 'year to date' column would be useful. Also, the margin obviously depends on the products sold to each of the customers. If Norrison buys something made uniquely for them, which other customers don't want, then high sales at a lower margin may be acceptable. However, the questions raised are perfectly valid and more information should lead to informed decisions about doing business with each of the customers.

Customer and product profitability

Following the same process as the sales and margin analysis, the profitability of each customer or product can be determined theoretically.

In practice, this involves allocating the more obviously relevant costs, like selling and distribution, to each customer or product. If a sales rep is dedicated to two accounts and he spends his time equally on each, allocate half of his cost to each customer. Transport costs are probably allocated on the share of sales total each customer has, which is as good an arbitrary way as any.

Generally, such a profitability analysis will stop there. Allocating further costs becomes a guessing game (unless the company is using Activity Based Costing). For example, carving up the administration costs between customers is likely to be done on some estimated basis and may cloud the issue. What the managers are really looking for is an indication of which customers and products are making the most significant contributions to the company's profitability. Armed with that information, they can decide how to proceed with each customer or product – whether to develop it, drop it or just leave it alone.

Overheads statements

From the Profit and Loss Account in the management accounts pack, a departmental manager can see how his total spend relates to his budget – is he over or under? But knowing that he is over or under is not enough – he needs to know in what areas the variance occurred.

An overheads statement for each department will provide that information. It is a list of the expenditure by type of cost, invariably from the classification used in the general ledger. This is a common format for an overheads expenditure statement, showing actual costs against budget with the difference (variance), for the period and the financial year to date.

	Overheads statement					
	July 2011 – R&D department					
	Month			Year to date		
	Actual	Budget	Var	Actual	Budget	Var
	(£)	(£)	(£)	(£)	(£)	(£)
Salaries	1,200	1,400	200	3,900	4,400	500
NIC	122	145	23	396	448	52
Pension	90	95	5	280	300	20
Stationery	250	100	(150)	400	320	(80)
Plant hire	120	80	(40)	600	250	(350)
Patents	2,500	1,000	(1,500)	4,000	3,000	(1,000)
Consultancy	400	0	(400)	900	0	(900)
Depreciation	450	450	0	2,000	2,000	0
Total	5,132	3,270	(1,862)	12,476	10,718	(1,758)

Overall, the R&D manager has overspent by nearly £1,800 against the budget in the year to date, but the detail contains some interesting points. The costs relating to salaries are all lower than budget – is the department understaffed? Has this led to the need to use consultants, the cost of which was not budgeted?

The patents cost highlights a common problem with comparing actuals and budgets – phasing. Usually budgets for overhead expenditures are set in total for the year – in this case patents £12,000 – and then phased into accounting periods, often just dividing by the number of periods. It can be done more accurately – electricity and gas costs tend to be higher in winter than summer – but for the sake of ease and convenience, it's often done by dividing the total for the year into equal shares. Yet the nature of patent fees means making occasional lump sum payments, whereas the budget is spread equally over the year. The current variance might be due to a timing issue and, no doubt, the R&D manager will defend the overspend by saying that the total will be back in line with budget by the year end. He may argue that he only needs one 'free' month, with no actual spend against a budget of £1,000, to be back in line.

Depreciation is for the fixed assets that the department uses – perhaps several PCs and various electrical and mechanical devices, which are as mysterious to accountants as ledgers are to engineers. If the depreciation is over budget, the manager might feel aggrieved – after all, he doesn't directly control the depreciation charge, although it is related to the cost of the fixed assets that the department acquires.

It should be confirmed that the costs on the overhead statement are based on accruals *and* invoices, not just invoices. So as long as the Accounts department is aware that the R&D boffins hired a milling machine in September, but the supplier hasn't invoiced for it yet, an accrual is made to put the cost in the correct accounting period.

Ratios for management

Just as there are ratios for use by those wishing to analyse the financial accounts of a company, so they can compare its performance with last year or with competitors, so there are ratios which can be used by the management. These usually compare figures with the budget or last year's performance – a stock turnover ratio of 4 may be good, bad or indifferent, but we can't tell unless there is a point of comparison. Some of the ratios are the same as those used in analysing the financial accounts:

* stock turnover
* debtors days
* creditor days.

Others can only be determined with knowledge of what is in the more detailed management accounts, rather than the summarized information shown in the published financial accounts.

Percentage margin by customer/product – although discussed previously, this ratio is repeated here for emphasis. The financial accounts give no details of sales by individual customer and knowing where the margin is being made can help managers determine where the focus of effort ought to be.

Sales per employee – this ratio can be worked out from the published accounts, since one of the notes to the accounts is the average number of employees during the year. However, the management can have this information on a monthly basis. It is more important in some industries than others, especially if the company has the ability to hire and fire temporary and casual workers.

Industry-based ratios – such as sales per square foot for retail stores. Unobtainable from the financial accounts, these ratios serve as comparison of efficient use of assets (floor space) between stores of the company and industry averages (often available from marketing data companies).

Added value – a statement of added value may appear in the published accounts. It is certainly often a key feature of the glossy brochures produced by plcs. Added value represents the wealth created by the company in turning purchased items into sold ones. Mathematically, it is sales less the cost of bought in goods and services.

The difference between added value and profit is all the other expenses – wages or salaries, interest, tax and dividends.

Added value can be used, alongside profit, as a measure of the company's ability to make a whole worth more than the sum of its parts – for example, a Jaguar is worth more than the individual elements of its engine, chassis, body, interior, etc.

Other information for managers

There is other financial information available which may be included in the management accounts pack, or reported separately, perhaps even on an ad hoc basis when required.

* Slow moving and obsolete stock items
* Overdue debtors listing
* Purchases by supplier
* Non-financial information i.e. sales and production data.

6

roles and responsibilities

Busy, busy people, accountants. The common misconception is that they just push through all the paperwork, sending invoices to customers, paying suppliers' invoices. Oh, there is so much more to it – true, those tasks have to be done, otherwise there are no supplies to make the goods they sell, and no money to pay for it all. But those Accounts don't produce themselves, and then there's the budget, the planning, and all those queries from the R&D manager wanting to know why he's overspent against his budget this month.

We might have looked at cash flow a couple of times before, but it is so important, it is definitely worth a bit more time. The point will be emphasized that everyone in a company has an effect on cash flow, and it really should not be left just to the accountants. It is all to do with working capital – if you control levels of stocks, debtors and creditors, cash control follows. Doing that takes good management. Informed management even, which might be you after you've read this.

Activities of an Accounts department

Different companies organize their Accounts departments in different ways, with some functions being the responsibility of other departments (sales invoicing and credit control might be under Sales; computers might be a separate department). However, by and large, the activities and responsibilities discussed in this chapter fall under the domain of Finance.

Sales ledger

Also known as *accounts receivable*, this function can incorporate up to three main areas: sales invoicing, sales ledger and credit control.

Sales invoicing

This prepares the sales invoices (based on despatch or delivery notes) to customers. These may be typed out from the delivery note details, or automatically issued by the computer system. Responsibilities would also include raising credit notes, having first verified the customer's claim for a credit (due to short delivery, rejected items or pricing error). Note that an invoice must contain a VAT registration number (if the business is VAT registered) and a date. It also usually indicates credit terms or the due date for payment. A credit note looks very similar, except it says credit note instead of invoice.

Sales ledger

This enters monies received (by cash, cheque or BACS direct into the bank) from customers against their invoices, reducing the amount owed. Payments from customers are usually accompanied by remittance advices (see below), which state the invoices that have been paid.

	Theodore Enterprises Limited	
	Remittance advice	
	Date of payment: 28/02/11	
Invoice No	**Date of invoice**	**£**
12545	12/01/11	4,212.00
12852	28/01/11	2,515.50
Total		6,727.50

The cheque for the payment may be printed as part of the remittance or separately. Alternatively, a simple piece of paper or a compliments slip bearing the same details as above will be sufficient to let the supplier know which invoices have been paid.

To assist customers, statements (see below) are often sent out to them each month, detailing the invoices still outstanding. Indeed, some companies insist on paying 'on statement' rather than 'on invoice', which means that they will pay out once a month only after they have received a statement.

Sunburst Formations Ltd
Statement of account

Customer: Stonesthrow Enterprises
Date: 31 March 2011

| Invoice | Date | Age of debt (days) | | |
		0–30	31–60	60+
6052	16.12.10			£512.35
7145	12.01.11			£440.25
7190	17.01.11			£244.16
8333	27.02.11		£812.66	
8739	03.03.11	£416.55		
8892	06.03.11	£446.32		
Total		£862.87	£812.66	£1,196.76

Some statements just list outstanding invoices; others, like the one above, 'age' them into columns. If remittances and statements cross in the post, the statement will be out of date and incorrect.

Credit control

This involves establishing credit limits for customers (through bank and trade references) and chasing customers for payment. The latter usually starts with a telephone call, then perhaps a polite letter and eventually court proceedings if the customer continues to avoid paying. In the meantime, Credit Control should have put the customer 'on stop' (refusing to accept further orders or deliver any orders in progress) to avoid any potential loss being increased by further sales.

The setting of credit limits is based on the risk of losing sales against the risk of the customer not paying. Information used to establish the limit includes past trading experience, bank references, trade references (from other suppliers to the customer) and instinct. It can, of course, also include an analysis of the customer's accounts!

The setting of credit limits for customers and the decision to put them on stop are normally both done in consultation with the Sales department. There is often a conflict between Credit Control, which wants to stop further supplies being sent to a customer due to non-payment, and the Sales department, which doesn't wish to lose an account. Resolution of the conflict often comes down to judgement, but the key maxim in this situation is that a sale isn't a sale until the money comes in. Actually, in strict accounting terms, it is a sale as soon as the invoice is raised, but from a money management view, anyone can sell to someone who isn't going to pay and it doesn't matter what price you got!

So, the basic tools for cash collecting are, firstly, a telephone and, secondly, information on outstanding debts. This information comes from the sales ledger, which lists for each customer the invoices and amounts outstanding, with due dates for payment. In essence it looks like a list of statements of account for each customer.

Purchase ledger

Also called *accounts payable*, this is the opposite side of the coin to sales ledger – dealing with suppliers. Suppliers' invoices are posted to the purchase ledger, after matching to a purchase order or delivery note, if such a system is used by the organization. If not, some other method of authorization is required, perhaps the signature of a sufficiently high-ranking manager. Suppliers also send statements that can be reconciled to their ledger accounts.

The purchase ledger is also the source of cheques, which are run periodically to pay suppliers. The usual routine is for the computer (or manager) to select all those invoices due to be paid by a certain date. The financial accountant, or whoever is responsible for determining how much is to be paid out overall, has the option to edit the list, usually deleting certain suppliers from it for a number of possible reasons:

* the invoices may be in dispute (e.g. due to poor quality of product);
* there may be limited funds available to pay out;
* the supplier may also be a customer with overdue debts.

When suppliers are chasing to be paid, Accounts will check that the sum claimed agrees with what is on the purchase ledger for that supplier. The supplier's statement of account can be used for this purpose.

Payroll

The level to which payroll is carried out by an organization varies from company to company. Some will even contract out the whole job to a bureau. Otherwise, the process can be taken from gross pay through to net pay and the paying of employees, or stop at any stage in between before it is handed over to an outside agency.

Gross pay is the total amount earned by an employee and is either hours worked times hourly rate or, for salaried employees, a fixed amount per month. On top of this, there can be numerous additions – overtime, first aid allowances, shift adjustments.

Of course, the total gross pay is not the amount the employee receives. Standard deductions are income tax (PAYE) and national insurance contributions (NIC). Further deductions are in the form of pension contributions, charitable donations, union dues and others.

All of which leaves a payslip looking like this:

Name A Zahar		**Payroll no.** 545	
NIC no. TT 45 25 37 A		**Tax Period** 6	
Tax code 350L			
	This period		Year to date
Basic pay	£1,000.00		
Overtime	£154.50		
Total Gross	£1,154.50		£7,422.65
Pension	£50.00		£300.00
Tax paid	£236.25		£1,280.00
NIC	£103.91		£668.04
Net Pay	£764.34		

Extra costs to the company are the employer's national insurance contributions (NIC), based on the employee's gross pay, and any pension contributions made by the company. All these figures need to be worked out – the source of data is a clock card for those paid by the hour. It is much easier if the rest is done by appropriate computer programs, although there are tables available to calculate manually the correct tax and national insurance amounts, depending upon the employee's gross pay.

Paying employees can be done by cash, bank giro transfer, BACS or, less commonly, by cheque. Giro transfer and BACS make the payment directly into an employee's bank account, while cash payments can be made by an outside firm for added security. Employees are given payslips to notify them of their earnings and deductions.

The payroll department works out the amounts to be paid to the Department of Work and Pensions (DWP)/HM Revenue and Customs for the NIC and tax deducted, plus the employer's NIC. This is paid monthly. Pension contributions are handed over to the pension fund managers (usually an insurance firm) according to stipulated frequencies, again usually monthly.

As well as answering the inevitable queries the payroll department also has a busy time at the tax year end (5 April). It does not matter when the company ends its fiscal year, the tax year end is a set date. The payroll prepares and issues a number of forms at this time:

* **P60/P14** – copies are sent to the employee and the DWP of employee's earnings in that year. Earnings are shown after tax deductible items, such as pension contributions
* **P35** – this is a summary of tax/NIC due and paid by the company
* **P11D** – an employee earning more than £8,500 is deemed by the government to be a higher-paid employee! Such employees may be assessed for benefits-in-kind or non-cash payments, the most common of which is a company car. The benefits have to be listed on a P11D

so that the tax authority can add them to its calculation of the employee's tax liability.

Cash book and petty cash

Receipts from customers and payments to suppliers, employees, government agencies – anyone – all have to be entered into the cash book. Every so often, at least monthly, the cash book is reconciled to the bank statement. There can only be two reasons for differences and they have to be identified item by item to achieve a full reconciliation:

1 **Unlodged receipts** – these are cheques and cash paid into the bank but not yet showing on the statement

2 **Uncleared payments** – are cheques which have been issued but that have not been presented or that have not cleared the bank account.

For example, here are the last few entries in the company's cash book:

		Receipts	Payments
Balance b/f		£54,312.44	
23/7/11	Aspar Gmbh	£5,000.00	
23/7/11	Bugaboo	£2,750.00	
24/7/11	Chasthom	£1,550.25	
24/7/11	Aqua (1054)		£4,680.00
24/7/11	Efferedy (1055)		£812.15
		£9,300.25	£5,492.15
Balance c/f		£58,120.54	

The latest bank statement looks like this:

	Debit	Credit
Balance b/f	£54,312.44	
25/7/11 Payments in		£7,750.00
Balance c/f	£62,062.44	

The reconciliation is:

Balance per bank statement	£62,062.44
Plus unlodged receipts	£1,550.25
Less uncleared cheques	£5,492.15
Closing balance	£58,120.54

This leaves cash book and bank statement in perfect harmony.

It may be that unlodged receipts have not been banked yet or that it takes a couple of days for them to appear on the bank statement. The principles are the same when you balance your personal bank account – you do it by considering any cheques issued that haven't yet cleared and any receipts not yet showing on your bank statement.

Petty cash is a relatively small amount of cash kept on site for minor payments (milk bills, vending machines) and sometimes employee advances or expenses. All payments should be backed up by receipts and expenses claim forms and summarized weekly or monthly for posting to the general ledger to account for the expenditure. The petty cash should be balanced at least monthly – the cash still in hand plus receipts and expense forms should equal the normal cash total. The petty cash amount is reimbursed on the basis of what has been paid out (backed by receipts), usually by a cash withdrawal from the bank.

Fixed asset register

It also usually falls to Accounts to keep a list of all the company's fixed assets, in the form of a register. It can be either a manual record or a computerized one. The entry for each fixed asset will record the following details:

* asset reference no.
* description
* date of acquisition
* supplier
* original cost

* date of revaluation
* revaluation value
* depreciation period (years)
* accumulated depreciation
* net book value
* date of disposal
* proceeds from disposal.

The accumulated depreciation amount is added to with each passing accounting period, with a corresponding reduction in the net book value (original cost less accumulated depreciation). It is the sum of these records which goes to form the figures in the fixed assets section of the company's Balance Sheet.

The general ledger

The most prominent function of the Accounts department – the one thing that everyone knows they do, even if they know nothing else about Accounts – is that they are the ones who produce the financial results.

The key to the financial and management information reporting is the general ledger. As well as producing the reports, the Accounts department must also 'maintain' it through journals, accruals/prepayments, reconciliation of control accounts and by creating new account codes to enable more accurate reporting.

Other activities

One of the advantages of accounting is that it requires involvement with all other departments, since these, between them, originate the causes of all transactions. This often gives the Accounts department an insight into the workings of other areas that surprises their colleagues. Hence accountants are usually represented on project teams, not just for their financial knowledge, but because they have a wider view and some understanding of the activities of other departments.

The Accounts department also produces cash flow forecasts, is heavily involved with budgeting and financial planning, perhaps even strategic planning. Any request for management information is normally directed at Accounts in the first instance and it is quite common for the head of the Finance department also to be responsible for the company's computer systems.

All in all, there are quite varied activities going on in the Accounts department.

Cash flow management

Practical management of the cash flow

Controlling the cash flow on a day-to-day basis is usually the responsibility of the financial director or the financial controller.

Money comes in from:
* debtors – which is determined by the level of sales and the credit terms given
* loans/share issues – which don't happen often and thus are not a daily concern for the management.

Money goes out to:
* creditors – set by how much is spent on stock and overheads, labour, fixed assets and credit terms
* statutory bodies – HM Revenue and Customs (VAT)
* employees – as their wages
* lenders/shareholders – in the form of interest, loan repayments and dividends.

There are two simple rules which are easier to state than follow. But, if adhered to, the rules will inevitably produce a growing pile of cash ready to spend in large amounts on fixed assets:

1 Sales revenues must be higher than all costs, which implies the company is in profit.
2 Goods and services must not be paid for until payment is received from the customer. This demands the co-operation of the supplier – imagine a nursery growing plants from seeds and cuttings. Until the plants have grown to a saleable size, then been sold and paid for, the company won't want to pay for the seeds. This could be months later.

An operating cash flow forecast, for use by the management, is more specifically related to real cash than the additions and subtractions of the formal Cash Flow Statement:

	Cash forecast for April			
Week number	*21*	*22*	*23*	*24*
Receipts:	£375,000	£212,000	£374,000	£240,000
Payments:	£	£	£	£
Wages/salaries	12,000	12,000	12,000	40,000
NIC/PAYE			20,000	
VAT	280,000			
Direct debits		5,000	2,000	6,000
Creditors	112,000	84,000	220,000	65,000
Total payments	404,000	101,000	254,000	111,000
Movement	(29,000)	111,000	120,000	129,000
Opening balance	82,000	53,000	164,000	284,000
Closing balance	53,000	164,000	284,000	413,000

The receipts from customers will be forecast by Credit Control using the sales ledger to estimate due payments. In this example, the payments to be made in week 21 surpass the collections, reducing the bank balance. The company (i.e. the manager responsible) might prefer to try to delay some of those payments until it receives money due to it later in the month, to maintain a safe balance at the bank.

Controlling working capital

Keeping firm control of the company's working capital has an enormously beneficial effect on the cash flow, and vice versa. The key to doing this comes from looking after the elements of working capital and managing them properly – it does not happen by itself.

Stocks
* Keep stocks as low as possible (not buying stocks means not having creditors to be paid).

BUT

* Beware of being overstocked, while avoiding stock outs and losing sales.

Debtors

* Have good credit control (see below).
* Remember that a sale is not a sale until it is paid for.
* Don't sell to anyone who won't pay!
* Keep customers to the terms.
* Shorter credit terms entitle you to get paid sooner.
* 'Early settlement' discounts may induce some customers to pay earlier than due, but they pay less for doing so.
* Get the paperwork right – invoice details must be correct to avoid delays in payment.
* Ask for payment! Make contact a couple of days before it is due to make sure there are no problems.
* Speak to the person who has the authority to arrange payment, not a clerk who can only pass the message on.

Creditors

* Get good terms – longer terms mean you don't have to pay until later.
* Try to arrange payment so that it follows receipts from customers.
* Do not abuse suppliers by making them act as a bank – what action do you take when your customers try to do the same thing to you?
* Prioritize payments if funds are limited (e.g. wages!).
* If purchases can be reduced, deferred or avoided, payment can be delayed or may not be required at all.

Credit control – getting the money in

The first task of Credit Control when faced with a potential customer is to establish a credit limit. This is usually done in conjunction with Sales which, in the normal scheme of things, would like a high credit limit to avoid lost sales. Ever cautious, Accounts will probably suggest a lower figure, wary of exposing the company to a potential bad debt (a customer who doesn't pay).

The credit limit can be based on a combination of trade references, bank references, a credit agency reference, Companies House reports (e.g. the latest statutory accounts), previous trading experience and the sales rep's personal knowledge of the company.

Once the account is up and running, Credit Control will monitor the customer's payment record. If invoices become overdue and persistent phone calls are not leading to payment, stronger action may be required.

Legal action can be threatened and enforced. In the meantime, the customer will be placed on stop, meaning that no further deliveries will be allowed. This often upsets Sales people who may be worried about offending the customer. Whether the account is reopened after payment has been made will be the subject of more debate between Accounts and Sales!

Factoring

One of the ways of improving cash flow is to factor debts. When this happens, the sale is made to the customer in the normal way. Then a factoring company pays the company immediately, usually about 80% of the invoice value. It has in fact 'bought' the debt.

The customer then pays the factoring company the invoice value, which passes it on to the supplier, less the 80% already advanced and its own fee, typically 5% to 10%. This can be an expensive way of doing business, but it does guarantee a swift income of cash after sales.

Credit insurance

Credit insurance is a way of insuring customers' debts, so that if a customer ceases to trade (i.e. goes bust), you can claim a percentage of the outstanding debt from the insurance company. Naturally, insurers don't like to cover companies that could go under, hence their scrutiny of the published accounts!

Like all insurance, there is a price to pay – but it's useful if you need it.

7

corporate
financial
planning

If depreciation causes managers to feel perplexed, mention of 'the Budget' can create fear! Yes, the accountants are often the ones who put it together, but they are not the ones who provide the source information. Sales managers will prepare sales budgets, production managers production ones, etc. It is worth these managers knowing how the budget is going to be used, and why it is sometimes a battle royal to get the final figures agreed. Strategic planning takes a longer view (budgets are usually for a year), and are often a bit more speculative. That is no reason for *not* doing planning: that would be a much bigger risk.

Failing to plan

There is an adage that 'failing to plan means planning to fail'. Successful companies do not amble along, suddenly finding themselves market leaders. The directors of these companies will have planned how this will have been achieved. Even though not all their ideas and strategies will have turned out in the way that they hoped or expected, at least they had some method in mind to achieve their goal.

The alternative to planning is to drift along aimlessly, reacting to whatever happens each day. Planning is a function that is often carried out with considerable assistance from the Accounts department, since they have access to much useful information.

Strategic planning

This takes a long-term view, typically five years ahead. Some companies go for ten years, but many of the assumptions about future market and operating conditions are subjective even at five years ahead, so beyond that the data becomes highly speculative. There are many theories of strategic planning, but most contain the following or similar elements.

Mission statement – this sets out what the company is about, what it stands for and what its values are.

Corporate objectives – given the company's mission statement, what are its objectives? These are not just financial – although making a profit is often an objective, it is usually not the only one or even the primary one. Other areas for consideration should include markets (which ones? what position in each?), products (which ones?), stakeholders (what are their objectives?), social (including environmental) issues, technological factors and the personal objectives of the management.

Internal and external analysis – if you want to get to Edinburgh, you need to know whether you're starting from Ipswich or Carlisle. Similarly, if the board wants to get the company to a position where it will have met its objectives, it needs to know where the company is now. Current financial status comes from the latest accounts, market shares are available from information bureaux (if not the company's marketing department) and evaluation of other parts of the business can come from a traditional SWOT analysis – strengths, weaknesses, opportunities and threats. Consideration of the external environment (competitors, suppliers, markets, etc.) allows the planning team to judge what might change in the future.

Strategies – after all the information is safely gathered, the hard part comes – working out how to get from the current position to the desired one. The strategies will drive the company forward to achieve the objectives and are usually broken down into functional areas – there will be strategies for marketing, production, sales, financial, personnel, R&D, etc.

The forward-thinking planner will also realize that some of the assumptions made about the future will not come to pass, so she will have in place contingency strategies. These are needed in case something goes wrong. Such disaster planning may include having action plans ready to cope with the loss of a major customer, destruction of a manufacturing site, the resignation of key personnel or changes in legislation affecting sales or production. Hopefully, these emergency plans will never see the light of day but, if the worst does happen, the management knows what to do immediately. Managers don't have to spend days considering their options while everything collapses around them.

Short-term goals – five-year plans are all very well, but they are actually achieved a day at a time. Consequently, the long-term strategies need to be translated into short-term goals, directing lower levels of the management to tasks which will, when aggregated over the five years, culminate in the successful achievement of the corporate objectives. Setting goals is also a good way of communicating to employees what the corporate objectives of the company are and how they can help achieve them. It won't be done without them.

Review and re-plan – the strategic planning exercise is an annual one, even though the plan itself covers five years.

This is because circumstances will not have turned out exactly as planned, nor will the company's performance have been exactly on target. It might even have been better than expected, leading to an upgrade in the objectives. So a review is carried out and the plan is revised if necessary.

The budget

The logical short-term translation of the strategic plan is the annual budget. Expressed in financial terms, it covers just a year. In theory, its achievement should keep the company on track to achieve its corporate objectives. The textbook term for this is 'goal congruence'. There are a number of important features of the budgeting process.

Top down or bottom up? – even though the budget should align with the five-year plan, how is it actually set? If senior management decides on the numbers ('We decree sales this year will be £12.5m.'), this is a top-down approach. It is then left to sales managers to decide how this target will be achieved and which products and customers will make up that total. Alternatively, if those who have to implement the budget are given the initiative to set their own and the figures are consolidated to a company total (subject to board approval), this is the bottom-up approach. In practice, the first is usually favoured since it is quicker, comes naturally from the strategic plan and, since the directors bear ultimate responsibility, gives them the final say.

Advocates of the bottom-up method point to increased motivation due to participation by lower levels of management, who may also produce more realistic goals being nearer the cutting edge. However, there are accusations of bias, as managers may seek to give themselves budgets that are easy to achieve, fearful of the consequences of not doing so.

There is also the problem of reconciling a bottom-up budget with the long-term goals. A bottom-up approach may yield a total of £10m sales when the board expects £12.5m to keep in line with its five-year strategic plan. It may require a number of reworkings to reach a compromise (or to find a way of making the £12.5m!).

Zero base approach – this is an alternative and imaginative way of budget setting. Instead of putting limits and conditions upon managers, this process gives them some leeway and asks questions such as:

* 'If the board wanted sales of £12m, how much would you need to spend on advertising? How many sales reps would you need and how much would you have to pay them?'
* 'To produce 400,000 units next year, how much material will you have to buy? At what cost? How many people would you need in each area of production?'

As its name suggests, this approach starts with only a few assumptions. It does not impose the condition that what we do now must be copied next year, but allows managers the creativity of developing new ways of reaching solutions. Its chief disadvantage is that it is a slow process. It is much quicker to determine next year's costs by adding 5% to this year's to allow for inflation and by assuming that the underlying activities will remain unchanged. On the other hand, zero base budgets require thought, research, preparation and the ability to challenge existing assumptions. All of which probably account for its limited use.

Use of budgets

Budgets can be interpreted and used in a number of ways:

* to control operations
* to motivate staff
* to plan.

Control

The principal use of budgets is as a control tool. Deviations from budget are reported back to the management (this is feedback) and lead to corrective action. The most common use of budgets by managers is to control. It is the heavy-handed use of budgets that puts the whole budgeting process in a bad light. Kelly remembers last year when the budgets come round again, and decides to pre-empt any problems by adding an extra 5% to his cost budget – just in case and to avoid any future unpleasantness. And so the function of the budget is undermined.

Yet control is an important function and budgets play a vital part in it. They provide the comparison of budget against actual and make any deviations obvious, allowing managers to take corrective action.

Motivation

Budgets can also be used to motivate staff – bonuses can be paid dependent upon performance relative to budget. The budget becomes a target to be achieved, possibly stretching the management to reach new goals.

Letting middle and junior managers be involved in setting the budgets they will have to work with can increase their motivation, if done properly. Refusing to discuss the budgets and merely imposing them at the start of the budget period can certainly decrease their levels of motivation too. An individual manager who has her actual results measured against that budget is more likely to feel that the budget is achievable if she had a hand in setting it in the first place.

The key words here are *responsibility* and *participation*. Responsibility is allied with *authority*. It is possible for a manager to be given responsibility for a budget for a cost, but have no authority over expenditure incurred. That is not sound practice, but it does happen. It is important to identify where both authority and responsibility lie, and to try to match the budget responsibility accordingly.

Planning

The budget is a plan, part of the strategic one. It represents the one-year plan consistent with the organization keeping on track to meet its longer-term objectives.

The budget is a formal plan. The budgeted Profit and Loss Account and the budgeted Balance Sheet show the financial position that the directors or shareholders would be happy for the organization to be in at the end of the budget period. Indeed, if the budget is a true plan, it is where they would *expect* the organization to be, all other things being equal.

In addition, if the organization has long-term (strategic) plans, the forthcoming year's activities should help towards achieving the objectives of those plans. It follows that the budget is the plan for that year to keep the organization aligned with its longer-term goals.

It is difficult for one set of numbers to achieve multiple objectives, which is one reason why budgets come in for some criticism. What is a plan to one manager becomes a rigorous target in the eyes of another. Top management may view the budget as the planned actual performance of the company. To others, it contains impossible targets to be achieved or goals for others to achieve. For most, it will be the benchmark by which their actions are measured, assessed and, quite frequently, rewarded too. One budget, therefore, attempts to fulfil a number of functions and this can give rise to conflict. The Finance director may consider it to be a plan and so commits capital expenditure on the basis of anticipated future cash flows. The Sales director may turn the sales part of the budget into targets for the sales force to reach. It is even likely that she will set the goals with the budget in mind during the budgeting process. The Production director monitors his maintenance budget costs, minimizing expenditure.

These multiple functions of the budget need not conflict, but they can do. The Sales director may feel that because of market forces, she needs to spend over the advertising budget to ensure sales are reached. In some companies, the reply will be 'It's not in the budget, so it can't be done.'

Spending more on advertising means the plan would not be followed precisely, but if she does not make the necessary expenditure above budget, targets will not be met and actual results will differ from the plan anyway.

Reality v. budget

Never forget that the budget is not reality. When the budget is set, it is usually between three to six months before the start of the financial year to which it relates. That means that half way through the year, the assumptions upon which the budget was based are a year out of date. All sorts of things could have happened which render the budget less meaningful – a competitor could have launched a new product, perhaps two major customers merged, currency movements may have forced up the price of material imports.

It is important to realize that the budget may be wrong in such circumstances and that the slavish addiction to it may lead to short-term gain but a poor performance in the long term. To achieve this month's budget, costs may be cut and sales achieved through giveaway prices, but these successes in the short term may have a disadvantageous effect in the following months or years.

Forecasts

Once the budget for the year is set, it is usually set in stone, and it is the first point of comparison for the actual results. But because environmental operating circumstances do change, enlightened companies also have interim forecasts – mini-budgets that are more up to date. These can actually be enhancements of the original budget and come in the form of:

* rolling budgets – these just keep adding on another three months to the end of the budget, so there is always a plan for the next twelve months ahead
* flexed budgets – for instance, if sales are 10% up against budget, other elements of the budget are 'flexed' in line with the increase, to give a reappraised budget in line with a driving figure
* straight forecasts – another set of revised figures for comparison with actuals.

The Accounts department often prepares many of the financial figures in the budgets and forecasts, usually with the managers who will be responsible for seeing that they are achieved.